"**O**ne expert says salespeople should put down their rifles and gun sights and pick up a hoe instead. Author Ivan Misner says word-of-mouth marketing is ... based on slow, nurturing care — 'more like farming than hunting.'"

*The Denver Post*

"**T**his gem of a marketing book explains how to grow your business in the toughest of times with the oldest, best, and most cost-effective marketing method in the world."

The Ten Best Marketing Books
*Marketing Power*

"**W**hile 'word-of-mouth advertising' may appear to be an obvious technique, Mr. Misner sets out to prove it's really the world's most effective yet least understood marketing strategy."

*Business Marketing*

"**T**he ideas in this book really work! After six months with a new company, I became the top leasing agent; within eighteen months, my salary increased by 50 percent; and before long, I was able to launch my own company."

Melodee Cole
President, Cole Financial Services

"**E**xcellent advice and guidance on planning and organizing one's word-of-mouth effort. A very useful roadmap."

Dan Gordon
Editor, *Owner Manager Magazine*

**"O**ffers examples to demonstrate the power of word of mouth, shows how to develop referral networks, suggests how to deliver a positive message, and lays out how to put together a W-O-M marketing plan. Recommended for small business, professionals, and salespeople."
BOOKLIST

**"A**n excellent step-by-step method of pointing out the different avenues of networking and how to achieve success with each."
Michael G. Beason
Chairman and CEO, Southern California Training
Council

**"W**ell written and informative. It has a cookbook approach to developing word-of-mouth skills."
Randolph Byrd
President and Publisher, *Upline: The Journal for Network Marketing Leaders*

**"H**elpful to those who are starting to build contacts as well as those who have well-established networks. It will be required reading for our managers and loan officers."
Barrett Andersen
President and Chief Executive Officer, First Federal
Savings and Loan Association of San Gabriel Valley

**"A** powerful, nuts-and-bolts approach for increasing business. It will propel you to new levels of success."
Garbis Der Yeghiayan, Ph.D.
President, Mashdots College, Pasadena, California

# THE WORLD'S BEST-KNOWN MARKETING SECRET

### Building Your Business with Word-of-Mouth Marketing

### (Revised Edition)

## Ivan R. Misner, Ph.D.

**Bard Press**

**AUSTIN**

# The World's Best-Known Marketing Secret (Revised Edition)
*Building Your Business with Word-of-Mouth Marketing*

Copyright © 1994, 1999, 2000, 2005, 2007 by Ivan R. Misner, Ph.D.

Bard Press
5275 McCormick Mtn. Dr.
Austin, TX 78734
512-266-2112
ray@bardpress.com
www.bardpress.com

A Paradigm Publishing Book

To order the book, contact your local bookstore or call 800-688-9394

ISBN  1-885167-37-7 (978-1-885167-37-8) trade paperback

*Library of Congress Cataloging-in-Publication Data*

Misner, Ivan R., 1956-
      The world's best-known marketing secret : building your business with word-of-mouth marketing / Ivan R. Misner. -- revised ed.
      p.      cm.
      Includes bibliographical references and index.
      ISBN 1-885167-37-7 (pbk.)
      1. Marketing.  2. Word-of-mouth advertising.  I. Title.
      HF5415.122.M573    2000
      658.8--dc21
                           99-24405
                                  CIP

The author may be contacted at the following address:

Paradigm Publishing
BNI Enterprises Inc.
545 College Commerce Way
Upland, CA 91786-4377
      800-825-8286 (outside So. Cal.), 909-608-7575 (in So. Cal.), fax 909-608-7676
      www.bni.com
      misner@bni.com

## CREDITS

Copyediting: *Jeff Morris*
Proofreading: *Deborah Costenbader*
Text Design/Production: *Jeff Morris*
Jacket Design: *Archetype, Inc.*
Index: *Linda Webster*

**First Edition**
First printing: August 1994
Second printing: September 1994
Third printing: December 1995
Fourth printing: August 1997

**Second Edition**
First printing: March 1999

**Revised Edition**
First printing: March 2000
Second printing: June 2001
Third printing: July 2002
Fourth printing: July 2003
Fifth printing: January 2005
Sixth printing: January 2007
Seventh printing: November 2007

## DEDICATION

*This book is dedicated*
*with love*
*to my wife, Elisabeth,*
*who often says,*
*"You make the living —*
*and I'll make the living worthwhile"...*
*and she does,*
*with each passing day.*

— Ivan Misner

# Contents

# Figures

◆

# Foreword

Y ou are holding the definitive, compact resource on word-of-mouth marketing by one of the world's foremost experts on the topic. Dr. Ivan Misner is, perhaps, too modest to refer to himself as such, yet a simple examination of the record supports the view that he is a pioneer in the field of business networking and word-of-mouth marketing.

In 1985, Ivan founded BNI — Business Network Int'l. It began when he assembled a group of friends in Arcadia, California, to exchange business referrals. There was some overlap in the professions represented by the people who attended. As a result, these people asked Ivan to start another group in Pasadena and promised to get twenty people to come to it. The overlapping occurred again in Pasadena.

Soon BNI had several chapters. In less than fifteen years, it has grown to thousands of chapters throughout North America, Europe, Australia, Asia, and Africa, with new chapters continually forming. As of this printing, members of BNI have passed over five million referrals to one another, producing more than $2 billion in business for the participants. Dr. Misner and BNI have been featured in major newspapers such as the *Wall Street Journal,* the *New York Times,* and the *Los Angeles Times,* among many others.

The secret behind BNI's rapid success is simple: if you want to get business, you have to give business. Members must faithfully attend the meetings and be prepared to share referrals with each other.

We are pleased to write the foreword to this book because we know from our own research the importance of networking and word-of-mouth marketing. Clearly, personal networking is the way that most successful business people pursue the marketing of their businesses. People with responsibility for getting business in organizations of all sizes will benefit from the know-how that Dr. Misner brings to them with this concise, authoritative book.

*The World's Best-Known Marketing Secret* is a veritable gold mine of information from the acknowledged master in the field. It's accurate, humorous, and right on target for the needs of today's business professional. Happy and prosperous reading!

> Paul and Sarah Edwards
> Coauthors of *Getting Business to
> Come to You, Working from Home,
> Teaming Up,* and other books
> Los Angeles, California

# Acknowledgments

I would like to acknowledge the directors and staff of BNI, as well as my wife, Beth Misner, who assisted me in the development of this book.

I would like to thank the thousands of entrepreneurs and executives, too numerous to mention individually, whom I've met over the years and whose stories and insights helped me formulate the principles of generating word-of-mouth business.

Finally, a special thank you to Ray Bard, Jeff Morris, and the staff at Bard Press for their commitment to excellence, their insightful understanding of the material, their expertise, care, and attention. Without their help, this book could not have been done.

Ivan R. Misner, Ph.D.
Upland, California

January 2005

# About the Author

**D**r. **Ivan Misner** is the founder and CEO of BNI (Business Network Int'l.), the largest business networking organization in the world. Founded in 1985, BNI now has thousands of chapters throughout North America, Europe, Australia, Asia, and Africa. Each year, BNI generates millions of referrals resulting in billions of dollars worth of business for its members.

Dr. Misner's Ph.D. is from the University of Southern California. He has written seven books, including *The World's Best-Known Marketing Secret*, his first bestseller, and the *Wall Street Journal* bestsellers *Masters of Networking* and *Masters of Success*. He is a monthly contributor to the Expert section of Entrepreneur.com and serves on the business administration faculty at Cal Poly University in Pomona, California, as well as the board of directors of the Colorado School of Professional Psychology.

Called the "Networking Guru" by *Entrepreneur* magazine, Dr. Misner is a keynote speaker for major corporations and associations throughout the world. He has been featured in the *Wall Street Journal, Los Angeles Times, New York Times, CEO Magazine,* and numerous TV and radio shows, including CNBC television and the BBC in London. He has twice been nominated for *Inc.* magazine's Entrepreneur of the Year Award.

Dr. Misner is on the board of directors of the Haynes Children's Center and is the founder of the BNI Misner Charitable Foundation. He and his wife, Elisabeth, live in Claremont, California, with their three children, Ashley, Cassie, and Trey. In his spare time he is an amateur magician and a black belt in karate.

# Get Rich the Old-Fashioned Way

*One Plus One
Equals Many*

## CREATING A SOLID BUSINESS STRATEGY

**T**his is not a "get-rich-quick" scheme or an "easy-money" program. It is instead a solid foundation for building any successful business enterprise. One of the important things I've learned over the years is that the secret to success — without a little bit of hard work — is still a secret! This book enables you to establish a plan for building a solid foundation for your business. Developing a word-of-mouth marketing program is an effective, potentially lucrative way of generating more business. It's not even hard work when you consider the alternatives:

1. Increase your advertising budget.
2. Develop an effective public-relations campaign.
3. Pick up the phone and start cold-calling.

The first two alternatives can be expensive; the third is time-consuming and frustrating. The structured word-of-mouth marketing program we're about to explore is a straightforward system that enables you to develop new business within your community or industry by connecting with your friends, business associates, peers, family members, and clients. Using a systematic and professional manner, you get them to talk about your business to others.

A structured word-of-mouth marketing program works by turning dozens of people into sales representatives for your company. A structured word-of-mouth marketing program is also personally empowering: it's one of the few things that you, or someone who works for you, can do (other than cold-calling) that directly affects your success. Why wait for people to walk in your door? Why sit idly by, hoping that your existing clients or customers will refer you to others? With a structured word-of-mouth program you don't have to wait for the results of your last PR campaign to kick in.

As you'll soon discover, a word-of-mouth program will give you control and allow you to take ownership for the business development of your company. Such a program has worked for thousands of people in all types of businesses and will work for you as well.

## WHO WILL BENEFIT BY READING THIS BOOK?

The first edition of this book was published to give you the basics for developing a comprehensive and structured word-of-mouth marketing program in any endeavor you may pursue. That edition won praise from many sources, made the

Schwartz bestseller list, and was named one of the ten best marketing books by *Marketing Power.*

Like that volume, this third edition of the book looks at word-of-mouth marketing from the perspective of the people in the trenches generating business for themselves or their company. It outlines the basic principles necessary to make it work, while offering you a specific action program that you can begin today. It is a hands-on, how-to book that will enable you or your staff to increase the amount of business you generate through the magic of word of mouth.

Part I lays the groundwork for understanding the power and importance of word-of-mouth marketing. Part II addresses the key factors involved in developing a Powerful, Diverse Network of Contacts. And part III discusses the essential components involved in providing a Positive Message, Delivered Effectively. The combination creates a prosperous word-of-mouth program, which is discussed in part IV. The final section, part V, brings you into the process with your own word-of-mouth marketing plan.

This program is geared specifically to small-business owners, private practitioners, and salespeople for small or large firms. It will also be of value, however, to senior-level managers who want to give their staff hands-on training for effectively developing a word-of-mouth marketing program within their company. In short, it works for solo entrepreneurs as well as Fortune 500 executives.

I am confident that the world's best-known marketing secret, word-of-mouth marketing, will make your job and life more enjoyable and more rewarding.

**Part**

**I**

# Word-of-Mouth Marketing

*The Oldest, Best,
Most Cost-Effective Way
to Build Your Business*

# PART I

### CHAPTER 1
Word-of-Mouth Marketing
*The Concept and the Attitude That Make the Difference*

### CHAPTER 2
The Best Way to Grow Your Business
*Advantages of Word of Mouth*

### CHAPTER 3
Hand-to-Hand WOMBAT
*Winning in Today's Business Jungle*

# Word-of-Mouth Marketing

*The Concept and the Attitude
That Make the Difference*

## THE WORD-OF-MOUTH PARADOX

**W**hat if there were a way to build your business year in and year out regardless of fluctuations in the economy or the activities of your competition? There is a way. It's called word-of-mouth marketing.

Word-of-mouth marketing is a paradox. It is truly the "world's best-known marketing secret." How can anything be the "best known" and a "secret" at the same time? Easy. Practically everyone knows how important word of mouth is, yet very few people really know how to develop it effectively. Therein lies the paradox. Virtually everyone recognizes the phrase and its importance to the average business person. Yet those same individuals are often far less clear on the specifics of harnessing this all-too-elusive commodity.

For a phrase that is so universally recognized, it is amazing that the concept is so little understood. As a businessman and educator, I can state with confidence that we are not teaching the next generation of business professionals about word-of-mouth marketing. Recently I was reviewing three large, well-respected college texts for a course I was teaching for the school of business at a university in Southern California. Each text exceeded 450 pages. Yet only one made any mention of word-of-mouth marketing, and even then it appeared as a passing thought (paraphrased to shield the guilty):

> A final note is required. . . . Don't neglect the value of free advertising that comes from word of mouth. Customers who are happy with you and satisfied with their purchases certainly will mention your company to their peers, neighbors, and relatives. Those who are unhappy are even more likely to talk about your firm.

Although I agree with the author's comments, it's hard to believe this is all that's said about word of mouth in a huge business text. Word-of-mouth marketing is the world's most effective, yet least understood marketing strategy. Although the concept of word of mouth is universally recognized among marketing experts, it is seldom covered in popular or instructional books on business marketing. Such books make a fleeting reference to the concept but almost never provide details on how you can actually develop good word of mouth for your business. The few authors who do mention it either fail to provide a clear, concise, well-structured plan for the typical executive or entrepreneur to follow, or they focus on such a narrow aspect of the process that readers end up concluding that word-of-mouth marketing is synonymous with providing good customer service, when it is not.

## THE W-O-M FACTOR

**G**ood customer service is a prerequisite for long-term business success, but good customer service alone will not develop the volume of business that can be generated by word-of-mouth marketing. The reason for this is something that I call the Word-of-Mouth Factor (or W-O-M Factor). The W-O-M Factor has three related parts:

- ◆ People are more likely to talk about your company when they are unhappy than when they are happy or satisfied.

- ◆ Therefore, good customer service generally does more to reduce negative word of mouth than it does to substantially increase positive word of mouth.

- ◆ Thus, to increase your business through positive word of mouth, you must do more than increase the quality of your customer service.

In essence, good customer service can reduce negative word of mouth, but to significantly increase your business volume you need to do more than increase the quality of your customer service. You need to be skilled at word-of-mouth marketing.

A study conducted by the White House Office of Consumer Affairs found that 90 percent or more of unhappy customers will not do business with the offending company again. It also concluded that each unhappy customer is likely to share his grievance with at least nine other people — and that 13 percent of unhappy customers will tell more than twenty people.

Other studies reach similar conclusions. A West Coast market research firm found that before they're finished, dissatisfied automobile customers tell twenty-two others about their experience. A Texas-based research firm discovered that dissatisfied bank customers tell eleven other people, each of whom in turn tells five others. In other words, one unhappy customer results in sixty-six others hearing about the dissatisfaction, and you can bet that the fifty-five people in the "second generation" hear a whopper.

Author Jerry Wilson calls this type of response the "Rule of 3-33." According to Wilson, for every three people willing to tell a positive story about an experience with your company, there are thirty-three others who will tell a horror story.

If all of this is even partially true, and I see no reason to believe otherwise, then good customer service, at best, helps reduce or eliminate negative word of mouth, while perhaps making a small contribution to positive word of mouth. Yet too many entrepreneurs, especially first-time entrepreneurs, believe that simply providing an excellent product or service ought to be enough to induce people to flock to their door.

## POWERFUL WORD OF MOUTH: THE FUNDAMENTAL STRATEGIES

According to popular business lore, somehow positive word of mouth about a business will circulate sufficiently among the right targets on its own. This is wishful thinking. The effect doesn't occur fast enough to enable a business to grow at a brisk pace. The inescapable conclusion to all this is that if you want to have a solid word-of-mouth-based business, you have to take steps to generate it yourself.

♦ *If you want to have a solid word-of-mouth-based business, you have to take steps to generate it yourself.*

Herein lie the two key strategies that are the major components of this book. In order for any successful business person to create a prosperous word-of-mouth-based business, he or she must accomplish two things:

1. Develop a Powerful, Diverse Network of Contacts.
2. Create a Positive Message, Delivered Effectively.

Later in this book I will outline the specifics of these two fundamental strategies in detail. First, however, it is important to gain a broader understanding of the environment in which you are attempting to build your business.

## TAKING CHARGE

The best word-of-mouth programs I've seen happen by design, not by accident or wishful thinking. Many business people view word of mouth somewhat like the weather: "Sure, it's important, but what can I do about it?" Based on more than a decade of research, observation, and practical experience, I've found that in addition to focusing on the important issue of customer service, the average business person has much to do in order to build a referral business.

Word of mouth can be planned and nurtured. Anyone, including business owners, entrepreneurs, sales representatives, staff employees, even individuals serving in a volunteer capacity in any field, can accomplish plenty with a well-structured and systematically executed word-of-mouth plan.

All too often I have seen business people waiting for business to walk through the door. They think because they are good at what they do, people should be flocking to them. I'm afraid the truth is, it doesn't work that way! You have to take charge, no matter what business you're in or how good you are, and bring the business in to you. I once saw a cartoon strip of two large, ravenous-looking vultures perched on a tree limb, overlooking a dry desert plain. After quite a while, one vulture turns to the other and says, "Wait for something to die? Hell, let's kill something!" So it is with word-of-mouth marketing. You can't simply wait for people to come to you. If you do, one of your competitors who also provides good customer service will most likely find them before they show up at your doorstep. If you want to succeed, you have to go get your business, or better yet, have someone else get it for you through referrals.

## SUCCESSFUL BUSINESSES NEED AN EDGE

It's no secret that the economy goes through cycles. Each time it takes a downturn, unfortunately, salespeople, business owners, and professional service providers feel the fallout. Data released by various sources, including the U.S.

Small Business Administration, American Entrepreneurs Association, and Dun & Bradstreet, reveal that more than 50 percent of all businesses close their doors within their first seven years.

During a recession, the rate of business failure rises more dramatically. Not included in the figure cited above are the departments, plants, or whole divisions closed by large corporations when times are tough. In today's ever-changing business environment, if you want to be successful you need to have an edge over your competition.

Finding a truly effective edge isn't easy, and most businesses rely on advertising in one or more ways. Open the Yellow Pages and you will see thousands of advertisements, representing almost every business and profession. In addition to using advertising to try to gain an edge over the competition, businesses also focus some of their efforts in direct sales by using someone (owner, salesperson, or employee) to actively seek customers in their target market.

◆ *If you offer the same products or services through the same means to the same targets as your competitors, it's difficult to gain an edge.*

However, if you offer the same products or services through the same means to the same targets as your competitors, it's difficult to get that edge.

Today's successful business professional needs an edge. This means that you need to be very creative in order to be competitive in today's marketplace. Creativity in marketing your business has become a basic tenet for today's successful company or professional practice.

Three store owners shared adjacent storefronts in the same building. Times were tough. In hopes of picking up sales, the store owner at one end of the building put a sign over his front entrance that said, "YEAR-END CLEARANCE!!!" At the other end of the building, a second owner responded with his own sign: "ANNUAL CLOSE-OUT."

The store owner in the middle knew that he had to act fast or he'd lose a lot of business. After careful consideration, he hung a larger sign over his front door that read, "MAIN ENTRANCE."

The moral of this story: You can't control the economy. You can't control your competition. But you can control your response to the economy. And you can control your response to your competition.

> ◆ *You can't control the economy. You can't control your competition. But you can control your response to the economy. And you can control your response to your competition.*

## YOUR RESPONSE TO THE ECONOMY AND TO YOUR COMPETITION

The first step in building a word-of-mouth-based business is to understand that you control your response to the things around you. I have traveled around the country giving presentations to thousands of business people on how to develop word-of-mouth business. On one trip I attended an after-hours business mixer in Hartford, Connecticut. At the time, this area was in a severe recession and the only topic of discussion seemed to be how bad business was. The whole affair was depressing because nearly everyone was obsessed with the problems of the economy and its impact on their businesses.

I was introduced to one of the many real-estate agents attending. Given the decrease in property values in the region, I was leery of asking this gentleman the standard "How's business?" question. I didn't want to hear yet another variation of how the world was coming to an end. He shared with me, though, that he was having a great year. Naturally, I was surprised, and asked, "You did say you were in real estate, didn't you?"

"Yes."

"We are in Connecticut . . . aren't we?"

"Yes," he said with a slight grin.

"And you're having a good year?" I asked.

"I'm actually having my best year ever!"

"Your best year!" I said in amazement. After thinking for a moment I asked him, "Is this your first year in real estate?"

"No," he replied with a laugh, "I've been in real estate for almost ten years."

I asked him why he was doing so well, given the conditions of the economy and the stiff competition. He reached into his pocket and pulled out a blue-and-white badge:

---

# I ABSOLUTELY REFUSE
# TO PARTICIPATE
# IN THE RECESSION!!!

---

"That's your secret?" I asked. "You refuse to participate in the recession, so business is booming?"

"That's correct. While most of my competitors are crying the blues about how bad business is, I'm out drumming up tons of business through word of mouth."

Considering what he said, I looked around the room and eavesdropped for a moment on people complaining about how slow business was. While nearly all were commiserating with one another, I concluded that very few were actually seeking new business. As a result, very little business was being accomplished. If you want to do well in business, you must understand that it does absolutely no good to complain to people about tough times. When you complain about how terrible business has been for you, half the people don't care and the other half are glad that you're worse off than they are!

A self-fulfilling prophecy on a mass scale can be hard to change. Attitudes are contagious, both positive and negative. Be positive; surround yourself with positive professionals.

I am convinced that if you want to stand out from your competition, the worst thing to do is to cry the blues along with them. My conversation with the successful Realtor reinforced my belief that your attitude affects your income!

♦ *Your attitude affects your income.*

While you cannot control the economy or your competition, like the Hartford Realtor and the store owner with the huge sign, you most definitely can control your response to the economy and to your competition. If you let outside forces paralyze your actions, you will fail.

As we'll explore throughout this book, one of the single most effective ways that you can take charge of your situation independent of the vicissitudes of the economy is to gain an edge over your competition by mastering the skills of word-of-mouth marketing.

## HOT TIPS AND INSIGHTS

**1** Good customer service in and of itself cannot match the volume of business that can be generated by word-of-mouth marketing.

**2** Good customer service helps reduce or eliminate negative word of mouth, while perhaps making little or no contribution to positive word of mouth.

**3** If you want to have good word-of-mouth marketing, you must generate it yourself. Too many entrepreneurs believe that simply providing an excellent product or service is enough to induce people to flock to their door.

◆ Your attitude affects your income. You can't control your competition, the economy, interest rates, government bureaucracy, and so forth. You can, however, control your response to such challenges.

### Chapter 2

# The Best Way to Grow Your Business

*Advantages of Word of Mouth*

## MARKETING REALITY CHECK

**R**eality-check time. How many ways are there for you to increase your business? Dozens? Hundreds? Maybe thousands? Guess again. Try four. That's right, there are only four main strategies that you can incorporate to increase your business. Don't believe me? Then read on.

First, you can *advertise*. Oh yes, I know, there are many different ways you can advertise. There's radio, newspaper, magazine, and direct mail advertising. You can advertise on billboards, TV, park benches, pens, balloons, or leaflets. If you feel really daring, you can even try skywriting. But when the dust settles and the smoke clears, it's still advertising.

I am not suggesting that you stop advertising. Depending on your product or service, many forms of it can be very effective for you. But it doesn't matter whether you're Procter and Gamble or the corner florist — you don't have an unlimited budget to spend on advertising. Therefore, you choose your advertising options according to a somewhat fixed budget, and off you go. The real question is "Does your advertising bring in all the business you need or would like?" Ask yourself, "Am I making more money than I want because of the tremendous amount of business that advertising has brought to me or my company?" If the answer is no, then you need to increase your advertising budget. If you can't increase your advertising budget, then you need to adopt another strategy.

> ◆ *It doesn't matter whether you're Procter and Gamble or the corner florist — you don't have an unlimited budget to spend on advertising.*

Competition for customers in our society is fierce. Your competitors are trying to win over the same clients or customers that you are. Even in a good economy, advertising does not guarantee success over your competitors. The people you're trying to reach, by some estimates, are bombarded by nearly two thousand advertising messages per day. This constant inundation means that your prospects potentially have many alternative sources of supply for the products or services you provide.

In a tough economy, advertising may not work at all. Especially when times are tough, you and your competitors are effectively competing for a reduced pool of available dollars, and people are more value conscious about the dollars they do spend.

Every business I've ever worked in, owned, or known has advertised in one form or another. Traditional forms of advertising, however, can be expensive. Based on a survey of major U.S. metropolitan newspapers, the average one-time cost in the year 2000 for a four-inch-by-four-inch display advertisement was $2,198.

If you were to run a $2,200 advertisement only once a week for one full year, you'd spend over $100,000. Assuming that the newspaper gave you a volume discount of 25 percent, you'd still spend over $75,000. For virtually all start-up companies, many companies that have been in business for a few years, and untold numbers of other long-established businesses, this kind of expense is not feasible.

What about advertising in a city or regional magazine? This is also not feasible for most businesses. A half-page, two-color advertisement in a local city or regional magazine, such as *Regardies* in Washington, D.C., *Boston Magazine,* or *Los Angeles Magazine,* runs $3,000 or more.

Television and radio are even more costly. A thirty-second, non–prime time TV spot in a

| Cost of a 4x4 Display Ad in Various Newspapers Across the U.S. | |
| --- | --- |
| Chicago | 3,900 |
| Dallas | 1,800 |
| Detroit | 1,960 |
| Denver | 800 |
| Hartford | 1,600 |
| Honolulu | 1,090 |
| Las Vegas | 650 |
| Los Angeles | 6,200 |
| Miami | 875 |
| New York | 6,600 |
| Phoenix | 825 |
| Portland | 925 |
| Seattle | 1,250 |
| Washington, D.C. | 2,450 |
| *Wall Street Journal* | 2,050 |

midsized metro area such as Memphis or Des Moines can set you back as much as $2,000 — for just one airing! Any type of consistent marketing effort using these media vehicles would require running your ad at least four to six times. The dollars add up quickly.

If you have the resources and have targeted your market appropriately, media advertising can greatly accelerate your plans. I suspect, however, that one of the reasons you picked up this book is that you're keenly interested in effective alternative strategies.

The second way to increase your business is through a *public relations campaign*. This can be very effective, but it can also be very expensive and time-consuming for a small company. Large companies hire PR firms to coordinate their public-relations programs. But this doesn't really help develop the credibility of the individual sales rep out in the field. Therefore, if your company is too small to hire a PR firm, or if you're a sales rep for a large firm, you need to create your own personalized PR program.

A good PR program can enhance your credibility, which in turn will have a positive impact on your word-of-mouth marketing opportunities. In chapter 7, I will discuss the importance of a good PR program to support your word-of-mouth efforts. However, it is important to understand that PR only lays the groundwork for a sale; it rarely closes the sale. While its importance shouldn't be underestimated, you should know that it rarely makes a quick difference in your bottom line. Therefore, no business can rely primarily on its public relations effort.

♦ *Word of mouth has long been recognized as the most cost-effective form of marketing a business can use.*

The third way to increase your business is through *word of mouth*. Word of mouth has long been recognized as the most cost-effective form of marketing a business can use. Tom Peters, author of *Thriving on Chaos*, regards word of mouth as one of the major ways a business can bring in new clients or customers. Peters asserts that one has to be "just as organized, thoughtful, and systematic about 'word-of-mouth' advertising" as with other forms of advertising and marketing. Yet, "you never see a 'word-of-mouth communications' section in marketing plans," he says. I, too, believe that if you don't have a well-structured plan, you're not likely to have impressive results. Many business professionals make the mistake of thinking that developing good word of mouth is about providing "good customer service."

## FOUR WAYS TO MARKET YOUR BUSINESS

| Marketing Strategy | Initial Goal | Ultimate Goal | Cost | Advantages |
| --- | --- | --- | --- | --- |
| Advertising | Create awareness and leads | Image in marketplace and sales | Big dollars for media | Target or wide coverage |
| Public Relations | Create awareness | Image in marketplace and some sales | Big dollars for public relations specialists | Wide coverage |
| Word of Mouth | Generate referrals | Sales | Staff time | Target or wide coverage; efficient, extended impact; inexpensive; quality customers |
| Cold-Calling | Generate sales through direct contact | Sales | Substantial staff time, shoe leather, and patience | ??? |

Unfortunately, as I said earlier, most marketing surveys have shown that consumers are ten times more likely to talk about you if they are *unhappy* with your service than if they are happy or satisfied. The best way to get truly impressive results is to have a plan and develop a structured program.

There's one other marketing strategy that a lot of people use as an alternative to advertising and PR, and that is, yes, that's right, the "C words" — *cold-calling!* Cold-calling — just mentioning it makes me shiver. Given the other options, who in his right mind would want to spend the rest of his professional life cold-calling?

Well, there it is, your marketing reality check. Given only these four strategies for increasing your business, I'd have to recommend advertising. However, most businesses have a limited budget to spend on advertising. PR is best used in conjunction with other marketing efforts. And I don't know about you, but many years ago I promised myself I would never do a cold call ever again for as long as I live! That leaves only one other way that you can effectively build your business: by word of mouth.

## A Cost-Effective Form of Advertising

**W**ord of mouth is a form of advertising and, like media advertising, requires careful planning to achieve a worthwhile return for your time and energy. As you begin to use and benefit by word-of-mouth advertising, you will see that it is a very cost-effective medium. If you haven't developed a structured word-of-mouth marketing program to generate referrals, then you can't enjoy its benefits.

While many business executives and entrepreneurs recognize the value of referrals to their respective organizations, they are not clear on how to consistently generate a large number of referrals. Worse, they don't realize that there is a segment of the population looking for their product or service right now.

## People Want Referrals

**P**eople don't want to go to the telephone book to pick a lawyer. People don't want to pick a real-estate agent from the Yellow Pages — or an accountant, or a chiropractor, or an insurance agent, or a dentist, or a mechanic. People want *referrals!* Historically, the only problem has been linking the people who need services or products with the people who provide them. A structured word-of-mouth campaign begins by acknowledging that there is a segment of the public that wants you and your service as badly as you want their business.

People from all walks of life want referrals — not just the business community, but the general public as well. Few people want to choose a dentist, for example, from a printed advertisement. People want to have more personal information before making such selections.

The general public have no idea what they are going to get when they hire someone through an ad. Years ago, a San Diego bank hired a private investigator to track down a bank robber and retrieve stolen funds. The search led to Mexico. The investigator crossed the border and then, realizing he would need a Spanish interpreter, opened up the telephone book and hired the first interpreter listed in the Yellow Pages.

> ◆ *There is a segment of the public that wants you and your service as badly as you want their business.*

After many days, he finally captured the bandit and, through the interpreter, asked him, "Where did you hide the money?" In Spanish, the thief replied, "What money? I have no idea what you're talking about."

With that, the investigator drew his pistol, pointed it at the suspect, and said to the interpreter, "Tell him that if he doesn't tell me where the money is, I will shoot him where he stands."

Upon receiving this message, the bank robber said to the interpreter, "Señor, I have hidden the money in a coffee can, under the fourth floorboard, in the second-floor men's room of the Palacio Hotel on Via Del Rio in La Paz."

"What did he say?" the investigator asked the interpreter.

"Señor," said the interpreter as he thought for a moment, "he says he is prepared to die like a man!"

Whenever you choose a professional exclusively from an advertisement and have no other source of information, you may be taking a big risk as to the quality of service you will receive. With referrals, the risk is greatly reduced. Someone else has done business with that person and is recommending that professional to you with confidence.

## REFERRALS ARE GOOD BUSINESS

**C**ompare a lead that you receive from an advertisement with a similar lead (that is, referral) that you get from someone you know. The referred lead is easier to close and costs less to obtain. Often, the referral provides a higher-quality client or customer with less chance of misunderstanding or disappointment. When I ask audiences why referral business is better than the business they get from ads, they say the referred business

- is easier to close,
- has far fewer objections,
- has a stronger sense of loyalty,
- remains a client longer, and most important of all,
- has a higher sense of trust.

Relying on the advice of a mutual friend or acquaintance, the referral starts with a higher level of trust for you and your product or service. Getting dozens of people to send such referrals your way every day — and this book will show you how — is what building a successful word-of-mouth business is all about.

## ADVERTISEMENTS THAT TOUT THEIR GOOD WORD OF MOUTH

**W**hy is it that while most businesses have some sort of plan for their advertising program, few have a plan for generating business via word of mouth?

Ironically, some companies focus on how effective word-of-mouth advertising has been for them — right in their advertisements. It's as if they were saying to prospective customers, "Most of the time, we don't need to pay for advertisements like this one because we get so many customers from word of mouth. Lucky for you we decided to run this ad, in case you don't know any of our current customers."

A radio ad I once heard was sponsored by a medium-sized commercial bank. In the ad, the bank asked the question, "Would you refer your bank to a friend?" They bragged that they got most of their new customers from referrals from their existing customers. This company recognized the value of their word-of-mouth business — so much so that they felt compelled to incorporate it into their advertising campaign.

Recently I heard another radio ad for a local business. They spent fifty out of sixty seconds discussing how important word of mouth was to their operations. During the last ten seconds, they announced that over 80 percent of all their business came through word of mouth, with the remaining 20 percent of their customers coming from "advertisements like this one!" Sometimes you wonder if such advertisers do have strong word of mouth or are just trying to cash in on the aura of having it.

> ♦ *Some companies focus on how effective word-of-mouth advertising has been for them — right in their advertisements.*

In this chapter I reviewed the four ways to market your business and the importance of a word-of-mouth-based business. In the next chapter, I'm going to show you how you can actually create your own word-of-mouth marketing plan in order to make the most effective use of this valuable concept.

## HOT TIPS AND INSIGHTS

**1** A structured word-of-mouth campaign begins with the understanding that there is a segment of the public that wants you and your service as badly as you want their business.

**2** Referrals are powerful because they reduce risk — for the customer and for the product or service supplier.

**③** A referral is easier to close and costs a lot less to obtain. The referral tends to be a higher-quality client or customer with less chance of misunderstanding or disappointment.

**④** Referred business is easier to close, has far fewer objections, has a stronger sense of loyalty, and remains a client longer.

**⑤** Some companies recognize the value of their word-of-mouth business, so much so that they talk about it in their ads.

**⑥** You cannot let word of mouth take its own course. You need a plan specifically designed to bring in referrals.

# Chapter 3

# Hand-to-Hand WOMBAT

## *Winning in Today's Business Jungle*

## PLANNING YOUR WORD OF MOUTH

**E**veryone knows it's a jungle out there; we're doing business in a very competitive environment. I often see three types of people in business: (1) those who make things happen, (2) those who wait for things to happen, and (3) those who say, "What happened?" Too many of the entrepreneurs and business professionals I've met never knew what hit them and were forced to go out of business. They were ill prepared for the daily challenge of bringing in new business. As we continue to move toward a global economy, marketing your business will not get any easier. Competition will spring from more places and directions.

You can talk about your enterprise; you can advertise, market, and promote it; but nothing will generate clients better than one person telling another that your business or service is the best in town. As we've discussed, you cannot let word of mouth take its own course. You need a plan specifically designed to bring in referrals.

---

♦ *WOMBAT: a way to create dozens of sales volunteers for your company, each carrying your business cards and recommending your services or products.*

---

Today, more than ever, successful business people need to use Hand-to-Hand WOMBAT (Word-of-Mouth Business Acquisition Tactics). This is a well-planned, well-executed word-of-mouth program that offers a way for you to replicate yourself. The system I'm going to lay out for you involves creating dozens of salespeople for yourself or your company, with each one of them carrying your business cards and recommending your services or products.

## TWO KEY STRATEGIES

T he balance of this book focuses on two key strategies you must incorporate into your business to make yourself a master of word-of-mouth marketing. With the approach outlined in this Hand-to-Hand WOMBAT Plan, you will immediately see a major difference in the word-of-mouth business that's generated in your organization. An effective Hand-to-Hand WOMBAT Plan incorporates the following strategies:

### A. Developing a Powerful, Diverse Network of Contacts

1. Determining your Contact Spheres, slaying old myths, expanding your spheres of influence, establishing

Strong and Casual Contacts, becoming a gatekeeper, and recognizing unexpected referral sources

2. Developing a reputation as a Hub Firm, avoiding the cave-dweller mentality, and understanding the difference between knowledge networking and referral networking

3. Diversifying your business networks — learning which groups to choose from, why diversifying is important, different types of organizations, and how to choose the right groups for you

## B. Creating a Positive Message, Delivered Effectively

1. Laying the foundation for your program, creating a desired image, acquiring networking skills, and developing incentives for people to refer you

2. Working your networks, preparing your introductions, mastering the business mixer, using the "Ten Commandments of Networking a Mixer," hosting your own event, and learning how to give and get referrals

3. Developing lasting relationships; farming, not hunting; keys to success in networking; and networking vs. notworking

It's easy to see that Hand-to-Hand WOMBAT involves a Powerful, Diverse Network of Contacts plus a Positive Message, Delivered Effectively, resulting in a prosperous word-of-mouth-based business. Each of these two strategies (A and B in fig. 3.1) represents one of the next two parts of this book. Together, they present a complete blueprint that will greatly enhance your ability to bring in quality business referrals through word of mouth.

> ◆ *Hand-to-Hand WOMBAT involves a Powerful, Diverse Network of Contacts plus a Positive Message, Delivered Effectively, resulting in a prosperous word-of-mouth-based business.*

**47**

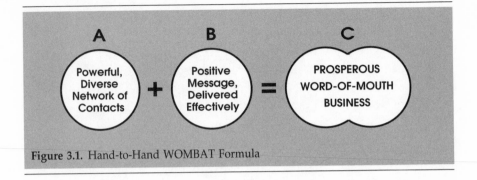

**Figure 3.1.** Hand-to-Hand WOMBAT Formula

## THE W-O-M GRID

**A**Powerful, Diverse Network of Contacts and a Positive Message, Delivered Effectively combine to produce a prosperous word-of-mouth business. As you can see in the W-O-M Grid (fig. 3.2), both are needed to create the desired result.

Having a Powerful, Diverse Network of Contacts without a Positive Message, Delivered Effectively would mean that, although you've established a solid network, you'll probably be unable to make effective use of the contacts you've worked so hard to establish. This is represented by the "5/1" relationship shown in the top left-hand corner of the grid. I call this type the "Schmoozer," because such an individual is good at talking and meeting people. Unfortunately, the Schmoozer's efforts tend to be unfocused because he or she hasn't developed a Positive Message, Delivered Effectively. The Schmoozer makes a lot of contacts, but not many sales.

On the other hand, if you create a Positive Message, Delivered Effectively but do not have a Powerful, Diverse Network of Contacts willing to refer you, your message will be falling on deaf ears, or worse yet, no ears. This is represented by the "1/5" relationship shown bottom right in the grid. I call this type the "Hunter," because he or she tends to be out looking to bag the big one. The Hunter has developed a positive message and can deliver it effectively, but hasn't taken the time necessary to develop solid, trusting relationships.

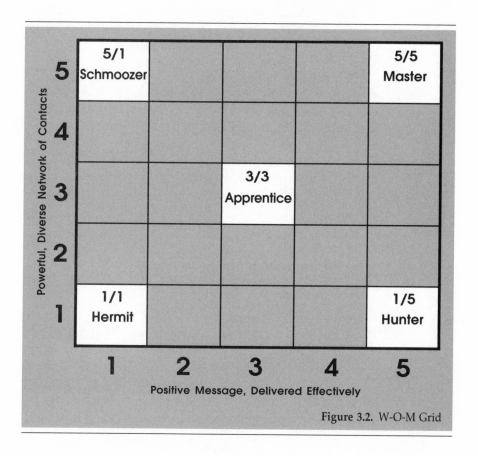

**Figure 3.2.** W-O-M Grid

Individuals making progress toward both ends would fall somewhere between "5/1" and the "1/5" points, as illustrated with the middle, or "3/3" grid point. These individuals, whom I call "Apprentices," are developing both strategies in a balanced manner but still have a way to go before getting a major part of their business through word of mouth.

Only when both a Powerful, Diverse Network of Contacts and a Positive Message, Delivered Effectively are successfully developed ("5/5" on the grid) can you realize a prosperous word-of-mouth-based business. Those who have achieved this I call "Masters" at word-of-mouth marketing, because with time and effort they have effectively combined the two key strategies of generating a referral-based business.

## HOT TIPS AND INSIGHTS

**1** Successful business people today use Hand-to-Hand WOMBAT (Word-of-Mouth Business Acquisition Tactics), a well-planned, well-executed word-of-mouth program that offers a way to replicate yourself.

**2** With two key strategies, you can become a master of word-of-mouth marketing and immediately see a major difference in the word-of-mouth business that is generated for you.

**3** Develop a Powerful, Diverse Network of Contacts by diversifying your business networks and determining your Contact Spheres.

**4** Create a Positive Message, Delivered Effectively by laying the foundation for your program, working your networks, and developing lasting relationships.

**5** Effectively combining the diverse network and positive message, as illustrated in the W-O-M grid, is the only way to develop a prosperous word-of-mouth-based business.

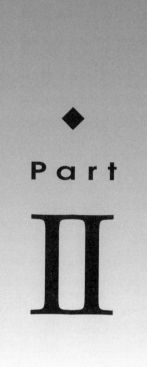

**Part**

**II**

# Developing a Powerful, Diverse Network

*Creating the Infrastructure to Promote Your Business*

# PART II

### CHAPTER 4
## Connections That Count
*Unleashing the Power of Your Rolodex*

### CHAPTER 5
## Making Your Company a Hub Firm
*Connecting with Other Networks*

### CHAPTER 6
## Six Kinds of Networks
*How to Choose Your Contacts Strategically*

# Chapter 4

# Connections That Count

*Unleashing the Power of Your Rolodex*

## THE "OLD-BOYS' NETWORK" AND OTHER GREAT MYTHS

I t's not that "old-boys' networks" don't exist; everyone knows they do. The myth is that you can't network unless you're in one! Old-boys' networks are no longer the only source of networking, and in many cases they're not even the best. Some of the male-dominated organizations that have been around for years were designed to be, or have become, passive networks. The members choose not to engage the potential networking ability of their groups.

> ♦ *It's not that "old-boys' networks" don't exist. The myth is that you can't network unless you're in one!*

By contrast, the women's groups created in the last two decades represent, for the most part, the beginning of the networking revolution. These groups made doing business the first priority at their meetings. In effect, they gave their members an opportunity to do business in a structured, professional environment. They made it acceptable to get together for no other purpose than to do business with and refer business to one another. As we know from the previous chapters, this phenomenon has now spread beyond "women-only" business groups.

Another great myth some people believe is that unless you graduated from the right university you will forever be left out of the choicest networks. Some well-known universities are renowned for networking but don't actually live up to their reputations.

Years ago, a friend of mine attended the doctoral program at a major private university in Southern California. On his first day, one of the professors spent nearly ninety minutes telling his students about the institution's old-boys' network and how it would open doors for them for the rest of their lives.

"Well," my friend recently said, "it's been almost ten years, and I still haven't received a referral from anyone in that class!"

It doesn't matter what school or country club you go to, passive networking yields passive results. Your school or country-club card alone won't get you business. What will build your word-of-mouth business is working your networks.

## EXPANDING YOUR OVERALL SPHERE OF INFLUENCE

T he foundation of any word-of-mouth marketing effort is people. Your sphere of influence represents the overall number of people with whom you network. These are people you know either very well or as casual acquaintances. To evaluate your sphere of influence, take inventory of the people you already know.

Many people have never established effective networking relationships with others they've known for a long time. Preparing your inventory is as simple as asking yourself, "Whom do I know?" or, "Who knows me?" This includes everyone with whom you interact or might interact, personally or professionally:

♦ Clients

♦ Business associates

♦ Vendors

♦ Creditors

♦ Employees

♦ Friends

♦ Family members

♦ Others

As you go through your software database, Rolodex, address book, and business-card box, discard the names of all the people who have moved on or with whom you've lost touch. Analyze your relationships with the ones you feel are still current. Ask yourself, "How well do I know them?" Then determine whether each individual is a Strong Contact (a close associate with whom you will network actively) or a Casual Contact (an acquaintance with whom you will network passively).

> ♦ *The more people you network with actively, the greater your sphere of influence.*

## ACTIVE NETWORKING AND PASSIVE NETWORKING

**A**ctively networking with others means you invite those people to one or more of the networking organizations to which you belong, carry several of their business cards with you all the time, and above all, refer them whenever you have an opportunity to do so. Active networking also means having a reciprocal relationship with others.

I prefer doing business with people who do business with me. Why give your business to someone who's not willing to return the favor? There are hundreds, maybe thousands, of competent, dependable business professionals in your area who provide any given product or service. They don't have to buy something from you to reciprocate. They can join one of your networking groups, carry your business cards, or simply refer you to people looking for your product or service.

Passively networking with others means that you use them as a resource occasionally but for some reason cannot actively network with them. It may be because they represent a narrow market where you have no way of assisting. Perhaps they've told you that they're not interested in participating in any networking organizations. Maybe they're located too far away to refer to them regularly.

## STRONG CONTACTS AND CASUAL CONTACTS

**I**t's important to have both Strong Contacts and Casual Contacts, but for different reasons. Strong Contacts usually are personal friends, close family members, partners, preferred clients, and close business or networking associates. They are people with whom you can actively network. Strong Contacts are willing to help you a great deal; however, they tend to represent closed circles — they don't change much, and they offer the same referrals again and again.

Casual Contacts are acquaintances, ex-colleagues, suppliers, and possibly some customers — people with whom you may passively network. Most people have many more Casual

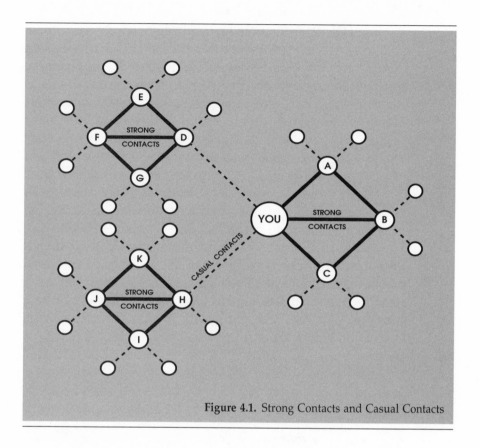

**Figure 4.1.** Strong Contacts and Casual Contacts

Contacts than Strong Contacts. Casual Contacts may not be willing to offer you a lot of assistance. However, they tend to belong to different circles than you. Thus, they can provide referrals outside your current sphere of influence and vastly increase your networking range.

As you can see in figure 4.1, by having a Strong Contact with persons A, B, and C, you have a connection with at least six other people. By having a Casual Contact with persons D and H, however, you have a connection, albeit weaker, with at least twenty other people.

◆ *Strong Contacts are personal friends, family members, partners, preferred clients, and close business associates with whom you can actively network.*

Strong Contacts provide higher-quality connections; Casual Contacts provide a greater number of connections. Ideally, you want to employ both Strong Contacts and Casual Contacts, because they have different things to offer. Strong Contacts offer loyalty and genuine interest; Casual Contacts offer greater exposure and provide networking bridges between clusters of other contacts.

♦ *Casual Contacts are acquaintances, ex-colleagues, suppliers, and others with whom you may passively network.*

With effort, you can sometimes transform a group of Casual Contacts into effective Strong Contacts by using a well-structured networking organization. When committed business professionals gather regularly in a structured environment, Casual Contacts have a way of evolving into Strong Contacts. The key is to participate in groups that are very focused on networking.

## CONTACT SPHERES

A subset of your Strong Contacts is what I call your Contact Sphere. This is a group of businesses or professions that can provide you a steady source of referrals. They tend to work in areas that complement, rather than compete with, your business (fig. 4.2). For example, if you were to put a lawyer, a CPA, a financial planner, and a banker in the same room for an hour, you couldn't stop them from doing business. Each of them has clients or customers that could benefit from the services of the others.

It's okay if Contact Spheres overlap a little — the process still works. Here are some examples of Contact Spheres:

- ♦ Business services: printers, graphic artists, specialty advertising agents, marketing consultants
- ♦ Real estate services: residential and commercial agents, escrow companies, title companies, mortgage brokers

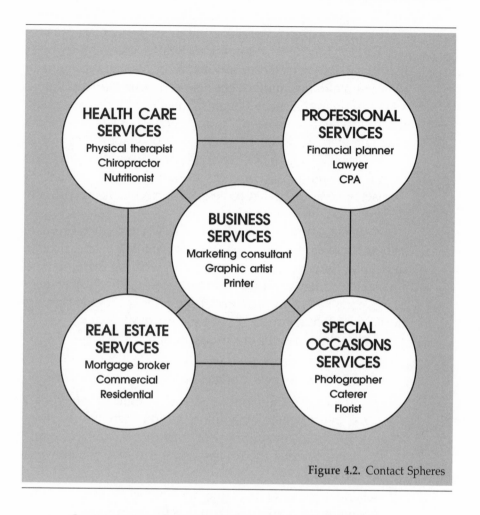

**Figure 4.2.** Contact Spheres

- Contractors: painters, carpenters, plumbers, land-scapers, electricians
- Health care services: chiropractors, physical therapists, acupuncturists, nutritionists
- Professional services: lawyers, CPAs, financial planners, bankers
- Business equipment vendors: telecommunications, computers, photocopiers
- Special-occasion services: photographers, caterers, travel agents, florists

In figure 4.2, each specialist in one of the Contact Spheres has a natural inclination to pass referrals back and forth with the others. Lawyers, CPAs, and financial planners continually refer people to one another because each works on a different aspect of the same client's financial needs. A florist gets many wedding clients, and hence is in a good position to refer a photographer and a caterer; when the photographer and caterer get wedding clients of their own, they are likely to reciprocate by referring the florist. In each case, the care and feeding of Contact Spheres by related professions increases the opportunity to receive qualified referrals.

Notice as well that referrals can flow naturally and easily *between* Contact Spheres. The florist's wedding clients may be in need of the services of a printer (for wedding invitations), a financial planner, or a residential real estate agent. Each of these professionals may, in turn, gratefully refer other clients to the florist who sent them good business prospects.

To get the most out of Contact Spheres,

1.  identify as many professions as possible that fit within your own Contact Sphere;

2.  identify specific individuals who could fit into your Contact Sphere by going to various networking organizations, consulting your card file or database, and reconsidering the professionals you may presently be referring;

3.  identify individuals in other Contact Spheres with whom you might exchange referrals; and

4.  invite each party to participate in networking groups with you so you can formalize your relationship.

At the end of this book you will find a Hand-to-Hand WOMBAT Plan that you can customize to fit your own needs. Utilize the concepts outlined in this chapter to complete the worksheets for your own personal plan.

While effectively developing solid Contact Spheres will increase your sphere of influence, it's not enough. Because Contact Spheres consist of small groups, you're not likely to gain exposure to a large number of individuals. Hence, pay attention simultaneously to your sphere of influence, Strong and Casual Contacts, and Contact Spheres.

## HOT TIPS AND INSIGHTS

**1** Old-boys' networks are no longer the only source of networking, and in many cases they're not even the best. The women's groups created in the last two decades give their members an opportunity to do business in a structured, professional environment.

**2** Your sphere of influence represents all the people with whom you network. These are people you know either very well or as casual acquaintances. The more people you network with actively, the more you increase your sphere of influence.

**3** Many people haven't established an effective networking relationship with others they've known for a long time.

**4** Preparing your inventory includes listing everyone you interact or might interact with, personally or professionally, including clients, business associates, vendors, creditors, employees, friends, and family members.

**5** Determine whether each person is a Strong Contact (a close associate to network with actively) or a Casual Contact (an acquaintance with whom you will network passively).

**6** Actively networking with others means inviting them to one or more of the networking organizations to which you belong, carrying several of their business cards with you all the time, and above all, referring them whenever you can.

**7** Strong Contacts provide better connections; Casual Contacts provide a greater number of connections. You want to use both, because they have different things to offer.

**8** Contact Spheres are businesses or professions that can provide a steady source of referrals for you. They tend to work in areas that complement, as opposed to compete with, yours.

**9** To get the most out of Contact Spheres, identify as many professions as possible that fit within your own Contact Sphere, identify specific individuals who fit, and invite each party to participate in networking groups with you so you can formalize your relationship.

### Chapter 5

# Making Your Company a Hub Firm

## *Connecting with Other Networks*

### HUB FIRMS

**D**eveloping effective connections with other business professionals is one of the cornerstones of building a word-of-mouth-based business. As a successful business person, you should attempt to develop your company into a Hub Firm. A Hub Firm is the key business in a constellation of independent businesses tethered to one another to make the most effective use of the organizational strengths of each. Cooperative relationships between these businesses can be the source of dramatic competitive strength. Generally the Cooperative Firms have a Contact Sphere (or symbiotic) relationship, as I described earlier. The difference here, however, is that one of the companies of this Contact Sphere, ideally yours, is the organizer or "hub" of the interrelated parties.

♦ *As a Hub Firm, your organization is the key link in a network of businesses that will substantially increase the number of referrals you will receive.*

As you can see in figure 5.1, the Hub Firm may work on various projects using different Cooperative Firms. For example, the Hub Firm might be working with Cooperative Firm 1 (CF-1) and Cooperative Firm 2 (CF-2). CF-1 and CF-2 might also need the assistance of Cooperative Firm A (CF-A). Thus, four firms — the Hub Firm, CF-1, CF-2, and CF-A — might all be working on one project together. In simpler terms, this might be something like a financial planner (the Hub Firm) working with an attorney (CF-1) and a CPA (CF-2), who have brought in a bank (CF-A) to assist a small business owner in a total analysis of his or her financial situation.

By becoming a Hub Firm, you make yourself and your organization the key link in a network of businesses that over time will substantially increase the number of referrals you will receive. This goes hand in hand with the notion of developing a Powerful, Diverse Network of Contacts.

## CAVE DWELLERS

T he process of developing your company into a Hub Firm begins with a concerted effort to develop connections with other business professionals. Gene Call, a trainer and consultant from Los Angeles and a good friend of mine, says

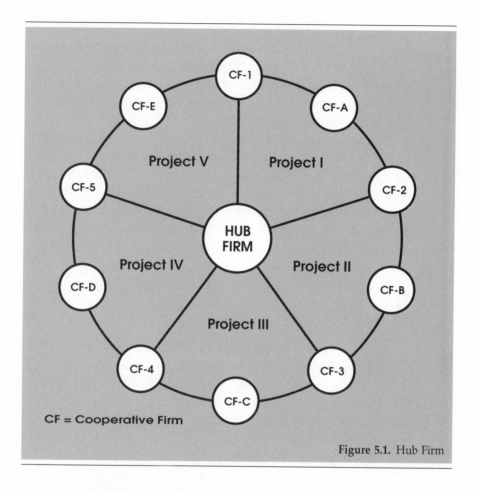

**Figure 5.1.** Hub Firm

that "most business people are cave dwellers. They spend their days going from cave to cave." In the morning they start off in their cave at home, get into a little cave with wheels (their car), and travel to a bigger cave (their office). They stay there all day long, get back into their cave-car, and drive straight back to their cave-home. The next day they do it all over again. The irony here is that these are the people who usually say, "Gee, I wonder why I'm not getting many referrals?" Just showing up for work is not going to build your referral business. I think Will Rogers said it best: "You might be on the right track — but if you're just sitting there, you're going to get run over!"

To break out of this cave-dweller mentality and become a Hub Firm, you need to begin evaluating the time you're spending in your caves and take a look at some effective ways to make successful connections. The best way I've found to make invaluable long-term business contacts is through business organizations or networks.

It's important to note that one type of business organization alone cannot fulfill a comprehensive word-of-mouth program, no matter how small or how large your operation. A good financial planner would tell you to diversify your investments, yet I consistently see business people investing their time and money in a single business or type of organization. I recommend that you join several different types of networking groups.

## A Caveat

**M**any people try to network under the false assumption that if they belong to, say, one Chamber of Commerce, belonging to three or four will bring them that much more business. However, you're likely to reach the point of diminishing returns quickly when you participate in several groups that are identical, or even similar.

So what groups are best for you? Start by taking a hard look at the business organizations you are in, or should be in. You, and if appropriate, your sales force, need to be out meeting people and establishing relationships.

## Knowledge Networking vs. Referral Networking

**M**ost people are involved in at least two types of formal networking groups. The first is intraprofessional networking, or "Knowledge Networking," as *Megatrends* author John Naisbitt calls it. Knowledge Networks foster self-help, information exchange, improved productivity and work life, and shared resources, according to Naisbitt, who cited networking as one of the ten megatrends impacting our society.

Organizations with a commonality of professional or personal interests, such as the American Society of Personnel Administrators, the Consumer Education Network, and the California Food Network, are all good examples of Knowledge Networks.

The second type of networking, and the one we'll focus on primarily, is interprofessional networking: multidisciplinary professionals and occupational types who network to increase each other's business. In fact, the primary purpose of most interprofessional networking groups is to increase one another's business through referrals.

In good interprofessional networking, participants get either the majority of their business or their best business through referrals. Organizations such as the Chamber of Commerce, Jaycees, Business and Professional Women, and Business Network Int'l. (BNI) are typical of groups in this category.

Different groups obviously offer different strengths and weaknesses in helping you generate word-of-mouth business. It's important to look closely at the makeup and structure of the various organizations that you might join before selecting those that best fit your needs.

If you haven't had much success in business organizations in the past, don't let that get in the way of doing what needs to be done to build your business through word of mouth today. This program will work if you follow it carefully. It works because it is based upon developing relationships with other successful business professionals.

The best way to begin the process is in a group or groups of other business professionals. The only alternative is to meet one person at a time, which inevitably means you're going to be working harder, not smarter.

The only people who are going to make referrals for you consistently are people who know you and trust you: your friends, associates, customers, patients, clients, peers, and family members. Strangers are not going to consistently give you business. You need to start spending time with the right people in structured professional environments.

## HOT TIPS AND INSIGHTS

**1** Join several different types of networking groups. Diversify your word-of-mouth activities.

**2** Develop your company into a Hub Firm, a firm that other companies rely on to coordinate efforts in providing effective services.

**3** Don't be a cave dweller. Get out and meet other business professionals in the myriad of business organizations that exist for that purpose.

**4** The only people who are going to make referrals for you consistently are people who know you and trust you. You need to start spending time with the right people in structured professional environments.

Chapter **6**

# **S**ix Kinds
# of Networks

*How to
Choose Your Contacts
Strategically*

## TYPES OF NETWORKING GROUPS

**T**here are at least six types of business organizations to consider joining (see box, next page). Depending on your time constraints, select at least three groups for participation. However — and this is critical — no matter what groups you end up participating in, remember something I've been teaching successful business professionals for many years:

It's not called "NET-SIT" or "NET-EAT," it's called "NET-WORK," and if you want to build a prosperous word-of-mouth-based business, you must "work" the networks that you belong to.

## CASUAL CONTACT NETWORKS

**C**asual Contact Networks are general business groups that allow many people from various overlapping professions. There are no restrictions on the number of people represented in any profession. These groups usually meet monthly and often hold mixers where everyone mingles informally. Casual Contact Networks may hold other meetings where there are presentations by guest speakers on important business topics, or to discuss issues concerning legislation, community affairs, or local business programs.

### TYPES OF NETWORKING BUSINESS ORGANIZATIONS

- ◆ Casual Contact Networks
- ◆ Strong Contact Networks
- ◆ Community service clubs
- ◆ Professional associations
- ◆ Social/business groups
- ◆ Women's organizations

The best examples of these groups are the thousands of Chambers of Commerce and similar groups active throughout the U.S. These groups offer participants an opportunity to make valuable contacts with many other business people in the community. They offer significant breadth to your goal of developing a word-of-mouth-based business because they enable you to meet hundreds of other business people.

Some people have told me that they did not get much business by "networking" in their local chamber. When I asked whether they attended mixers *regularly*, sat on any committees,

## A LOOK AT THE CHAMBER OF COMMERCE

The United States Chamber of Commerce, the world's largest business federation, represents an underlying membership of over three million businesses and organizations. It is organized on three levels: local, state, and national. On the national level, the Chamber of Commerce helps develop local and state chambers and represents national business interests to the federal government.

State chambers coordinate local chamber programs and represent the state business community to the state government. Information on small-business programs in the state is available through the state chamber. Local chambers serve the local business community with programs in economic development (hint: mixers), community and human resources, and public affairs.

The Chamber of Commerce Small-Business Programs Office serves as a central clearinghouse for information on getting started in business, expanding business overseas, and managing a business. The State and Local Chamber List includes a complete list of state and local chambers that have small-business and expert assistance programs.

attended the networking breakfasts, met with the executive director, or volunteered to be a Chamber Ambassador (a position that requires little work but provides much exposure) they always said "No." Well, guess what — networking is a contact sport! If you want to build your business through word of mouth, you must be willing to get out of your cave and make ongoing, effective contact with other busi-

♦ *It's not NET-SIT, or NET-EAT, it's NET-WORK — you must "work" the networks you belong to.*

ness people. Just being a member is not enough. You must make meaningful contact with the other participants, as regularly as possible.

By attending chamber mixers, presentations, and other activities, you can make initial contacts that will be valuable in other aspects of developing your referral business. You can find your local chamber by calling information in your area or by contacting the U.S. Chamber of Commerce:

U.S. Chamber of Commerce
1615 H Street NW
Washington, DC 20062
202-659-6000

## STRONG CONTACT NETWORKS

S trong Contact Networks are groups that meet weekly for the primary purpose of exchanging referrals. They often restrict membership to only one person per profession or specialty and tend to be more structured in their meeting formats than Casual Contact Networks. Their meetings include

◆ open networking,

◆ short presentations by everyone,

◆ a longer, more detailed presentation by one or two members, and

◆ time devoted solely to passing business referrals.

Such organizations require a far greater commitment from their membership. They usually have a set agenda, with part of the meeting dedicated to actually passing referrals you've picked up for members during the previous week. A good example of this type of organization is BNI, a group I founded in 1985 that is now one of the largest of its kind.

Strong Contact Networks provide highly focused opportunities for you and your associates to begin developing your word-of-mouth marketing campaigns. You won't meet hundreds of business people in this type of group, but all the members will be carrying your business cards around with them everywhere they go. The net result is like having up to fifty salespeople working for you! With a program like this, you will be

## A Look at BNI (Business Network Int'l.)

BNI was created in 1985 as a way for business people to generate referrals in a structured, professional environment. The organization has grown to thousands of chapters worldwide and has generated millions of referrals for its members.

The primary purpose of BNI is to pass qualified business referrals to the members. This is accomplished by developing strong business relationships within each chapter. Each chapter follows a structured agenda that includes presentations from the members and distribution of qualified business referrals at each meeting. These referrals are tracked and recorded by the chapter officers in order to gauge the activity and success of the chapter.

The chapters are supported by local directors who receive a 500-page manual and many hours of training before managing an area. Marketing materials, training, regular newsletters, meeting stimulants, chapter tool kits, and assistance from the local director and main office are but a few of the support services that members receive.

establishing powerful long-term relationships that will prove invaluable. I highly recommend that you join one such group.

Don't divide your loyalties. People who join more than one Strong Contact Network are promising their commitment to too many people. When other members discover that you've made the same commitment to people in a different group, they will eventually feel betrayed and will stop giving their business to you.

Because most Strong Contact Networks allow only one person per profession, people who belong to two such networks and get a referral for a profession represented in both networks will have to do one of two things: give the referral to only one, which effectively reduces by half the number of referrals they hand out in either group; or worse yet, give the referral to both, with each member believing he or she is getting a good referral, which would not be the case.

Select a network with a national or international base. I've seen literally hundreds of local independent groups open and close in less than a year because they lacked structure, support, and effective policies. Such groups generally turn into coffee klatches. They may look attractive at first because they don't have a lot of requirements and are inexpensive or free; but remember, in the long run you get what you pay for.

> ◆ *Don't divide your loyalties. People who join two or three Strong-Contact Networks are promising their commitment to too many people.*

Several marketing books of late suggest that you assemble a local network on your own. That is an excellent suggestion, if you have lots of time on your hands and enjoy administrative tasks. Otherwise, don't reinvent the wheel. There are several groups that have been around for years that provide support and are readily available. Plug into one that's done most of the work for you already. Most important, choose one that is well supported and isn't going to fall apart next month.

Strong Contact Networks focus on relationship-building in a professional environment. If you're interested in finding out more about a networking group like this, call or write BNI and ask for information on a chapter near you:

BNI — Business Network Int'l.
545 College Commerce Way
Upland, CA 91786-4377
800-825-8286 (outside So. Cal.)
909-608-7575 (inside So. Cal.)
www.bni.com
bni@bni.com

## Community Service Clubs

Community service clubs give you an opportunity to put something back into the community where you do business while making valuable contacts and receiving good PR to

## A Look at Rotary International

Rotary, the world's first service club, can be described in many ways. Functionally, Rotary is an association of local clubs gathered into a larger organization called "Rotary International." The individual member is a member of his local club; all clubs are members of Rotary International.

Officially, Rotary is defined as "an organization of business and professional men and women united worldwide, who provide humanitarian service, encourage high ethical standards in all vocations, and help build good will and peace in the world."

Specifically, a Rotary Club is composed of business and professional men and women in a community who have accepted the "ideal of service" as a basis for attaining fulfillment in their personal, vocational, and community lives.

Now about 1.2 million service-minded members belong to more than 29,000 Rotary Clubs in almost 160 lands. Clubs meet weekly, usually for breakfast, lunch, or dinner.

(Source: *Focus on Rotary*, by Rotary International)

boot. Community service clubs can be a fairly good source of word-of-mouth business. Such groups exist primarily to serve the community; however, they can also provide an excellent opportunity for business people to meet regularly and develop relationships.

Although there is almost no overt networking, long-term friendships, which are critical to the success of a solid word-of-mouth-based business, are established. Good examples of these groups include Rotary, Lions, and Kiwanis Clubs. In many ways, community service clubs were the original networks. The oldest, Rotary, was established in 1905 by Chicago lawyer Paul Harris with the idea that one person from each profession would belong and members would, among other things, help each other in business.

Originally Rotary was "to promote the scientizing of acquaintances as . . . an aid for success," but this early credo was dropped long ago. Although Rotary Clubs, as well as the other major service clubs, are now focused primarily on providing public service to their local communities, business is definitely conducted with fellow members. Today there are thousands of Rotary Clubs throughout most of the world, with both men and women members.

Service clubs, in and of themselves, do not offer great opportunities to get immediate business, and if you attend with that in mind, the members will not embrace you with open arms. People join and attend with the primary goal of giving back to the community. Nevertheless, as a by-product of their long-term associations with one another, members of service clubs accrue business referrals and other business benefits.

## MAJOR COMMUNITY SERVICE ORGANIZATIONS

Rotary International
1560 Sherman Avenue
Evanston, IL 60201
847-866-3000

Optimists International
4494 Lindell Boulevard
St. Louis, MO 63108
314-371-6000

Kiwanis
3636 Woodview Trace
Indianapolis, IN 46268
317-875-8755

Lions
300 22nd Street
Oak Brook, IL 60521
708-571-5466

The clubs routinely are populated with the movers and shakers in the community. If you're a member long enough, you end up befriending people who can open doors, present little-known opportunities, and help you run your business more effectively. Let me share two poignant anecdotes.

I had been a member of a service club for about two months. At one luncheon meeting, the club president announced that a community center project in town was short on funds and that the fundraising committee was seeking donations to finish construction. It seemed like a highly worthwhile project, so I got out my checkbook and began to write a check for fifty dollars. As I was writing, the president introduced two members of the club, both seated at my table, who had just donated $50,000 each! I closed my checkbook and slipped it back into my coat pocket very quietly. I didn't want anyone at the table to see that I had been writing a fifty-dollar check, when two of them had just donated a combined total of $100,000. At that very moment, I decided that these were very nice people to be having lunch with on a weekly basis.

Years later, when I had developed strong relationships with various members in this service club, I was lamenting to some of the members at my lunch table how I couldn't get a good mortgage rate on a particular property I wanted to acquire. One fellow at the table said to me, "Well, how much are you looking for?"

"One hundred fifty thousand dollars," I said.

"I've got $150,000," he replied. "When do you need it?"

"Are you kidding me?"

"No, I'm serious. I've known you a long time and I have some money that I can invest. When do you need it?"

"Next week would be okay," I said.

"Okay, fine. We can draw up an agreement next week."

"Will there be any points?"

"No, no points," he said. "Not amongst friends. Tomorrow we can work out the details."

The following week, we wrote up an agreement, and I had the money, just like that. Well, I really shouldn't say "just like that," because I had laid the groundwork with several years of participation in this service club. As one of his committee chairmen, I had helped this individual when he was club president, and we got to know one another during this time. If that hadn't happened there would be no chance he would have trusted me enough to loan the money.

♦ *Making effective contacts is a journey, not a destination. It is not something you do for a while and then stop.*

With any business organization, but particularly with service clubs, it is very important to remember that making effective contacts is a journey, not a destination: it is not something you do for a while and then stop; it is a process that you must continually follow.

For sure, this book is about marketing your business, but you also need to run your business, and your networks will support you in that capacity as well. In the box on page 76 are the addresses and phone numbers of a few of the major community service organizations.

## PROFESSIONAL ASSOCIATIONS

Professional associations, or what John Naisbitt calls "Knowledge Networks," have existed for many years. Association members tend to be from one specific type of industry, such as banking, architecture, personnel, accounting, or health. The primary purpose of a professional association is to exchange information and ideas.

Your goal in tapping into such networks is to join groups that contain your potential clients or target markets. A simple procedure for targeting key groups is to ask your best clients or customers which groups they belong to. This will give you an immediate list of at least three to five, and probably as many as ten to twelve, groups from which to choose.

Your best customers retain membership in the associations that offer the greatest value or for which there is some key strategic or competitive advantage. Similarly, the prospects you wish to target may, in many ways, operate like your best customers and have many of the same needs.

Joining such a group is like being a kid in a candy store; all that business is potentially within reach. Many groups, however, limit their membership to those who have specific industry credentials, and vendors aren't welcome (i.e., if you want to join an association of accountants, you have to be an accountant).

To generate more income or to give their full members a well-rounded slate of potential vendors, a growing number of professional associations have created an "associate member" category. The associate member may not be active in the business or profession for whom the group was formed.

In associations that allow vendors as members, you're likely to encounter considerable competition. Many people have the same idea that you do. Sometimes full members are turned off because they have been approached by so many vendors.

If you join a group that represents your profession (and not your target market), you can still make contacts that might lead to shared opportunities with people in your profession who have a slightly different specialty or need assistance on a large project. You never know where a good referral might come from, so don't ignore this as a possible opportunity.

At the very least, a professional association of peers enables you to evaluate the marketing materials and presentations of others. By taking a good look at what works for others, you may be able to improve your own brochures, cards, or presentations.

Some examples of professional associations are these:

◆ American Society of Personnel Administrators

◆ Certified Life Underwriters Association

◆ National Association of Professional Organizers

◆ American Bar Association

◆ American Medical Association

◆ National Speakers Association

Two directories found in the reference section of any library provide the names and addresses of thousands of professional and trade associations throughout the United States: *National Trade and Professional Associations* and *Gale's Encyclopedia of Associations*. Another common reference tool is the *Directory of Conventions*, which provides the names, addresses, and phone numbers of specific groups that have scheduled conventions up to two years in advance. The directory is arranged geographically and even lists the numbers attending.

Locally, you can tap into the vast reservoir of the professional luncheon circuit through the business-calendar section of your local newspaper. Such calendars provide the names of groups that are meeting, the location of the meeting, the cost of the luncheon, the topic for the meeting, and either the name of the meeting planner or a number to call.

## SOCIAL/BUSINESS ORGANIZATIONS

**E**ach year, more groups spring up that serve as both business and social organizations. Groups such as the Jaycees and various singles/business clubs openly combine social activities with business or networking, giving you an opportunity to combine work with a little pleasure.

One group I encountered claimed to be an "exclusive business and social network for successful single professionals." Unfortunately, my experience is that some groups tend to resemble an upscale singles bar as much as a networking organization. One woman told me that "if someone is more interested in finding a date than doing serious business, then these nooky networks [her term, not mine] are what they want."

Not all social/business groups are like this. If you are interested in combining work with social activities, I recommend the Jaycees. They tend to be very focused and professional. They may be reached at the following address:

Jaycees
Box 7
Tulsa, OK 74102
918-584-2481

## WOMEN'S BUSINESS ORGANIZATIONS

**W**omen's business organizations have been instrumental in shaping the nature of contemporary networking organizations. With the proliferation of women business owners in the 1970s and '80s and the difficulty they had in joining the "old-boys' networks" in place, many women formed structured, well-organized groups that met to network and provide professional support. These groups were created not as service clubs but as bona fide networking organizations. Many made no pretenses; the members were there to network, and everything else was secondary.

# A Look at NAWBO

Services of the National Association of Women's Business Organizations include counseling and technical assistance at the local level, primarily through networking with local members; holding monthly programs to address problems for the female business owner; and sponsoring an annual national conference that provides management and technical assistance training through workshops and seminars.

NAWBO is a dues-based national organization representing the interests of all women entrepreneurs in all types of businesses. It is affiliated with the World Association of Women Entrepreneurs in twenty-three countries.

Membership in NAWBO offers opportunities for members to expand their business horizons to national and international levels. Among the member benefits are local, national, and international networking opportunities; regional retreats, seminars, and training programs; educational programs, workshops, and seminars; international trade missions; and local, national, and international leadership and managerial opportunities. State chapters of NAWBO also offer many opportunities to make new business contacts.

Women's business organizations are very diverse in their structure and makeup. The one thing they have in common is that they tend to be concerned with education and professional development as well as networking. Some are Casual Contact Networks; some are Strong Contact Networks. Others are industry-specific professional associations, such as Women in Construction. The benefits of membership depend on the type of group you join.

For many women, such groups can be an excellent and nonthreatening way to increase their business. Surprisingly, many women's organizations allow men in their membership. Assuming the man conducts himself professionally, he can truly benefit from membership and participation because he'll be more widely recognized within.

An excellent example of a national women's business organization, and one that I recommend, is the National Association of Women Business Owners (NAWBO), which consists of more than forty local chapters and several thousand members nationwide. NAWBO helps female business owners expand their operations and represents women's business interests to federal and state governments. To learn more about NAWBO, contact them at this address:

NAWBO
8405 Greensboro Drive, Suite 800
McLean, VA 22102
703-506-3268

Other excellent women's groups include the following:

American Business Women's Association
9100 Ward Parkway, P.O. Box 8728
Kansas City, MO 64114-0728
816-361-4991

Business and Professional Women/USA
1900 M Street, NW, Suite 310
Washington, DC 20036
202-293-1100

## CHOOSING THE GROUPS BEST FOR YOU

**D**espite all that we've covered thus far, some people tell me they simply don't have time to go to business meetings regularly. I understand that objection well. If you feel this way, let me suggest that you throw away this book, pick up your telephone, and start making cold calls instead. Or, if you prefer, open your checkbook and start writing checks for more advertising. If you're serious about developing word-of-mouth business, there is no quick fix; you must meet people in a planned and structured way.

Which groups should you join? Don't let chance decide where you're going to spend your time and effort. Remember, the key is to *diversify your activity*. Don't put all your eggs in one basket; one type of business organization won't serve all your needs. Consciously select a well-rounded mix of organizations, with no two of the same type. If you have associates, partners, or employees, consider their participation when deciding which groups each of you will target.

## WHAT IF YOU WORK FOR SOMEONE ELSE?

Persuade your employer that you will get business by working with these groups. I met a bank manager several years ago who worked hard at persuading his supervisor that participation in BNI would yield substantial results for his branch. The supervisor reluctantly agreed to let him join on a trial basis. The manager began getting referrals soon after joining.

After several months, another member gave him a particularly good referral — a man who was disgruntled with the level of service at his current bank. The manager decided to visit the man at his company. The man told the bank manager that he felt he was not getting personal service from his bank.

The manager assured him that *his* bank prided itself on service. He gave the man his personal pager number and home telephone number and told him that if there were a problem he could be reached any time of day, at home or at work. The man thanked him for coming to his office and told him he would get back to him.

Two days later, at 9:00 a.m., the man was standing at the bank door with several savings and checkbooks in hand. The manager met him at the door and thanked him for coming to the branch. The man said he was impressed with the way he was handled by the manager and that he had decided to transfer his accounts to the manager's bank. To the astonishment of the bank manager, the new customer handed over checking, savings, and money-market accounts totaling over $950,000! After everything was completed, the man told the manager how glad he was to be referred to him by their mutual friend.

I first heard this story when my office started getting phone calls from every branch manager in Southern California who worked for that bank. Each of them wanted information about local chapters of BNI. When the bank manager who got the $950,000 referral told his supervisor where he got the referral, the supervisor (Remember him? The reluctant one?) called all his other branch managers and told them to join a local chapter of their own within the next two weeks.

♦ *Whether you are self-employed or work for someone else, start looking for groups that refer you new business.*

If you work for someone else, the lesson here is to persuade your supervisor. Not long ago, I spoke to an individual who wanted to join a networking group but was told by his boss that the company wouldn't pay for it. This savvy salesman asked his boss, "If I front the money myself and get two referrals that turn into sales within the next thirty days, would the company pay for it then?" The boss said, "Sure, if you come in with two sales, I'll see to it that the company pays for the membership." Well, guess what? This salesman, thus highly motivated, closed three sales and was working on four others at the end of the first thirty days. He told me that his boss "gladly paid for the original membership, and recently paid to renew it." Whether you are self-employed or work for someone else, start looking for groups that refer you new business.

## Selecting Your Networking Groups

The networking groups you choose to participate in will directly affect the success of your word-of-mouth marketing effort. The following five activities will help you get your networking off to a good start.

First, determine the types of organizations that you would like or need to join (see box, p. 70). Make sure to have a good mix (for example a Casual Contact Network, a Strong Contact Network, and a service club). Participate in at least three groups, but don't join more than one of each type.

Second, evaluate the potential networking organizations in your area that fit the profile you are looking for and select some to visit.

Third, visit as many of them as possible, and depending on the type of group, consider the issues listed in part 6d of the Hand-to-Hand WOMBAT Plan (p. 196). These questions are very important in your selection of a networking group.

Fourth, talk to members of each organization you visit and get testimonials on how it's been for them.

Fifth, go back to visit again. One time may not be enough (except for Strong Contact groups that may have your profession open at that moment — in that case, you may want to join before someone takes your spot).

## IF YOU SNOOZE, YOU LOSE

If you visit a group that allows only one person per profession and you like the group, and your profession is open, don't hesitate! I kicked off a chapter of BNI (which allows only one person per profession) several years ago in Hartford, Connecticut. At the end of the meeting, two real-estate agents were talking to each other at the back of the room.

I went up to them and asked if one of them planned on joining. They knew each other fairly well and one guy looked at the other and asked, "I don't know, how about you, are you going to join?"

"Well, I haven't decided," responded the associate. "I need to think about it. How about you?"

"I haven't decided, either," responded the first real-estate agent. With that, he told us he had an appointment, said his goodbyes, and left.

No sooner had he crossed the threshold than his friend announced, "I've thought about it and I think I'll join!" He immediately filled out an application and joined the new chapter.

Thirty minutes after the meeting, I received a phone call from the first agent. He said, "I've been thinking about it and I decided that I should join before Charley changes his mind and decides to join."

"Gee," I said, "I don't know how to tell you this, but old Charley waited about as long as it took you to get out the door to fill out an application."

"That dog!" said the frustrated agent. "I guess I've learned that you can't *blink* if you want an open spot."

That experience immediately reminded me of a story I once heard about two friendly competitors who, walking through the woods one day, rounded a corner and came face to face with a huge grizzly bear. The bear was standing on its hind legs, growling and snarling. It stood over seven feet tall, looked like it weighed a thousand pounds, and was not very friendly.

One of the walkers very gently lowered his pack to the ground. Slowly, so as not to startle the bear, he opened the pack and pulled out a pair of running shoes. As he started to lace up the first shoe, his companion whispered, "You know, that bear looks as fast as he is strong."

"I know," said the man, as he finished the first shoe and began with the next.

"I've heard grizzlies can top thirty miles an hour over short distances. You can't possibly outrun him," said the other man.

"I know that, too," said the first man as he finished lacing up the other shoe.

"If you know all that," continued his friend, "Why are you bothering with those sneakers?"

"Because," said the first man, as he turned his back and looked over his shoulder at his associate, "I don't have to outrun the bear, I just have to outrun you!"

The lesson behind these two stories is that if you find a Strong Contact group that you like and it has an opening, you'd better not blink or your competition will outrun you.

## FIND THE TIME

S ometimes people tell me they don't have time to attend business organizations but really need to generate some more business. To this I say, "No problem. Simply increase your advertising budget by a factor of X, or hire people to start making cold calls for you, and you won't need to go to any of those darn meetings."

Find time to leave your cave and meet other qualified business professionals regularly,

♦ *Networking is a contact sport! If you don't develop effective relationships, you can't possibly create a powerful, diverse, reliable network of contacts.*

or you'll never develop a prosperous word-of-mouth-based business. Networking is a contact sport! If you don't develop effective relationships, you can't possibly create a powerful, diverse, reliable network of contacts.

## YOUR HAND-TO-HAND WOMBAT PLAN

A s I cover the key concepts for you to build a prosperous word-of-mouth-based business, you should review the appropriate section of the Hand-to-Hand WOMBAT Plan (p. 193) and personalize it to fit your own needs. In other words, create your own custom word-of-mouth plan.

In selecting your business groups, first outline the groups to which you and/or your associates now belong, using the Hand-to-Hand WOMBAT Plan. Then list the groups in which you are not active, but that you would like to visit. Of these, which ones can you visit immediately? Which do you need to research for additional information?

For the ones that require more research, find out when and where they meet, then schedule those you want to visit during the next two to six weeks. With each group, consider the factors I discussed earlier.

Once you've visited all the organizations on your list, select the ones that you want to participate in. Make sure that it is a well-diversified list and that you are not in two groups that are similar.

## POWERFUL, DIVERSE NETWORK OF CONTACTS

**P**art II of this book has discussed the key elements relating to establishing a Powerful, Diverse Network of Contacts. This process includes determining your Contact Spheres, expanding your spheres of influence, establishing Strong and Casual Contacts, becoming a gatekeeper, working on becoming a Hub Firm, avoiding the cave-dweller mentality, and most important, diversifying your networks. If you do all these things, you will make great strides toward developing your referral-based business.

However, these elements are only half the effort needed to be successful at developing a word-of-mouth-based business. The first part of this book has walked you through the organizational part of your endeavor. The next section, part III, will take you through the key elements of implementing the contacts you will develop as a result of following the information outlined in this section.

As you advance through this book, refer to your Hand-to-Hand WOMBAT Plan in the back of the book so you can create your own personalized word-of-mouth program relating to the development of both your Powerful, Diverse Network of Contacts and your Positive Message, Delivered Effectively.

## HOT TIPS AND INSIGHTS

◆ Strong Contact Networks are groups that meet weekly for the primary purpose of exchanging referrals. Their meetings tend to be well structured and include open networking, short presentations by everyone, more detailed presentations by one or two members, and time devoted solely to exchanging business referrals.

**2** Community service clubs give you an opportunity to put something back into the community where you do business while making valuable contacts and receiving some good PR to boot. They can be a good source of word-of-mouth business.

**3** Your goal in tapping into professional associations is to join organizations that contain your potential clients or target markets.

**4** Women's business organizations have been instrumental in shaping the nature of contemporary networking organizations. Many groups are established as bona fide networking organizations; the members are there to network, and everything else is secondary.

**5** Don't let chance decide where you're going to spend your time and effort. If you have associates, partners, or employees, consider their participation when deciding which groups each of you will target.

**6** When evaluating groups, find out when and where they meet, then schedule those you want to visit during the next two to six weeks.

**7** For each group, consider these issues: How long has the group been in existence? What is the basic philosophy of the organization? How many members does it have? What is the quality of the membership? How does the cost compare with other forms of marketing? How often does it meet? How do other members feel about the group? What is your overall impression of the group?

**8** Using the Hand-to-Hand WOMBAT Plan in the back of this book, customize your own word-of-mouth marketing plan.

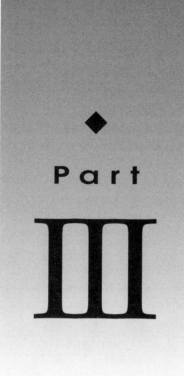

**Part**

# III

# Creating a Positive Message, Delivered Effectively

*Turning Positive Word of Mouth into Hot Referrals*

# Part III

### Chapter 7

# Positioning for Power

*Tools and Techniques to Enhance Your Business Image*

## IMAGE

T he first order of business in creating a Positive Message, Delivered Effectively is deciding what you're going to be, what you're going to offer, and to whom you're going to offer it. Let's explore how you create an image that will work for you around the clock.

"The age of image is here. From corporations to individuals, the impact of image is irrefutable," says Jeff Davidson, author of *Marketing on a Shoestring*. We show our desire for image enhancement on many levels; seminars on grooming, speaking, interpersonal communications, negotiations, video appearances, and wardrobe management are thriving. Why?

According to trainer and image consultant Mona Plontkowski, the reason for this increase is that "as we have shifted from a manufacturing environment to a service-oriented society, what consumers now pay for is often intangible. The image of a company and the people who work for it has taken on new importance in buying decisions. A reassuring, professional image makes people feel more secure when buying something they can't see or hold in their hand, like a service."

Because we are constantly bombarded with information and images through our daily work lives, travel, and television, our minds have learned to assimilate these stimuli quickly, rightly or wrongly make snap judgments, and move on. "The success of your business, whether large or small, often depends upon how you position yourself and what you project," says Davidson.

## CREATE AN IDENTITY

**P**ositioning can help you create an identity and maintain a secure spot in the minds of those you wish to serve. The concept of positioning was popularized in the early 1980s by Al Ries and Jack Trout. They observed, "In our over-communicated society, very little communication actually takes place." A company must create a position in the prospect's mind, recognizing that the most effective communication occurs when optimally placed and timed.

Being the "first" remains one of the quickest and easiest ways to gain a position in someone's mind. Who was the first person to walk on the moon? If you said Neil Armstrong, you are correct. Now, name any of the astronauts who walked on the moon's surface on the other five NASA moon missions. Not so easy, is it? If you're like most people, you probably have no idea.

When you are properly positioned, you save time, because others quickly understand what your company represents and offers. With positioning, each networking encounter, advertisement, message, employee, and every square inch of floor or office space contributes to the delivery of a consistent theme to the target market.

The identity you develop may be right only for you and for no one else. You may become the leader in an emerging industry, or a highly successful alternative to the leading company. You may be the only store open for twenty-four hours or the most exclusive shop in town, exhibiting wares by appointment only. In the highly competitive, swiftly changing environment that we exist in today, creating an identity that sticks in the mind of others is no longer optional but essential.

One way of creating an identity is to address issues of importance to the people you wish to serve. For example, in figure 7.1 you see an article I wrote for a business magazine about using word-of-mouth marketing in a recessionary economy. Articles like this help you establish your professional credibility, enhance your reputation, and of course increase your business.

## Obtaining PR

In our media-oriented society, your survival and growth in business are often based on how you appear in print. Pick up your area's business magazines or even the business section of your daily newspaper. Every issue of these publications carries an interview with or feature on a corporate executive or local entrepreneur.

Most of these stories are placed by public-relations firms that have been paid by the subject of the story. The profiles you see are part of a coordinated effort undertaken and funded by the company or individual publicized. The people or companies being featured are paying for it, or sometimes generating it themselves with a concerted in-house PR effort.

INDIANAPOLIS
# C.E.O.

**NETWORKING**

BY IVAN R. MISNER

# Surviving the Squeeze
# of a Tight  Economy

*In a slow economy, your business may depend on word-of-mouth advertising.*

It's no great secret that the economy goes through cycles. Unfortunately, each time it takes a down turn, the fallout is

*Ivan Misner has published numerous management and networking related materials including the book Networking for Success, How to Become a Notable Networker and his audio cassettes, The Ten Commandments of Networking and The Secrets of Notable Networking. In 1985, Misner founded the Network, which currently has more than 100 chapters.*

felt by sales people, business owners and private practitioners alike.

According to the American Entrepreneurs Association (AEA) more than 50 percent of all businesses close their doors within the first two years of operation. During a recession this number is known to dramatically increase.

Why do some businesses fail and others don't? I believe the answer is simple. If you have an edge you'll stay in business when times are tough.

Your competitors are in the market place right now trying to get the same clients and customers you have or want. In a tough economy traditional forms of advertising may not be enough.

However, most businesses need to advertise before, during and after a tight economic period. Studies show that companies which advertised strongly through the last recession came out of it with much greater percentages of their market share than before the recession. But, during a tight business economy, you must do something extra. Something your competition doesn't do.

That edge I'm referring to is building a solid word-of-mouth base that can carry

you through difficult economic times.

Occasionally, I meet people that feel that word-of-mouth is a little like the weather—sure, it's important, but what can you do about it? Well, according to Tom Peters, the author of *In Search of Excellence* and *Thriving on Chaos*, "you can be just as organized, thoughtful, and systematic about word-of-mouth advertising" as you are about your other forms of marketing.

With this in mind, I have created what I believe are the four essential steps to developing a word-of-mouth based business.

1. Write a 60-day "word-of-mouth" marketing plan.
 •What organizations do you want to participate in?
 •What professions do you need to begin networking with?
 •Which individuals do you need to connect with?
 •What incentives can you offer employees/clients/customers to develop a stronger word-of-mouth base?
 •What specific results do you wish to realize as a result of this plan?
2. Devote at least 50 percent of your marketing effort (dollars and time) to

developing a structured word-of-mouth network.

3. Make a true effort to refer other people. Remember "givers gain," those who give business to others, receive it in return.

4. Work "The Network." The secret to success without hard work is still a secret. Networking is not the same as "notworking."
 •Set lunch meetings with other members of your chapter.
 •Prepare for your presentation.
 •Utilize handouts to go with your presentation.
 •Develop special offers to members, if possible.
 •Meet all the visitors that come to your chapter.
 •Be an active participant—network!

The cold hard fact is that many sales people, business owners and professionals are going to go out of business in the next 12 months. You don't have to be one of them.

In a 1989 survey of more than 300 members of The Network, we discovered that their business increased by an average of almost 41 percent through networking!

In addition, 73 percent of the members in the survey said they closed large or substantial sales, clients, or customers through word-of-mouth networking.

These people have an edge. They have a solid word-of-mouth base, and they know how to use it. In a tight economy, your business may depend on that edge.

It's been said that "it's not what you know, but who you know." I don't quite agree. You see, it's not really what you know or who you know, but how well you know them that makes the difference.◊

For information on **The Network**, contact the Main Office at **(800) 825-8286** outside Southern California or **(714) 624-2227** in Southern California

**Figure 7.1.** Article in *Indianapolis CEO*

Suppose you're a remodeling subcontractor in Spokane and the city council has voted to restore a historic building. One well-placed interview on the significance of this structure to the community is likely to catch the eye of hundreds of builders and developers, preservation groups, historical societies, and anyone else concerned with architecture or historic preservation.

Consider a Richmond, Virginia–based hardware store owner who wanted to increase his visibility in the community and attract new business. To highlight and promote his line of products, he announced that he would sponsor an urban sculpture contest in which participants would use only junk hardware parts. He had "in progress" and "completion" photos taken. A PR agent was hired from the outset to ensure maximum exposure. A few weeks after the entries were judged, a major story appeared in one of the region's most prestigious monthly magazines under the by-line of the publicity agent.

To the average reader — indeed, even to the average marketer — it appeared that the publication either contracted with the writer to produce this story or accepted the piece "over the transom." Because publishers have long known of the healthy number of entrepreneurs in their community who wish to be written about and who have the funds to commission an article, publishers often get their material for free.

## THE VALUE OF FREE PR

**T**he manner in which the name and the products of the supplier are publicized does not appear to be advertising — rather, articles of social or community interest. "An article is far more influential than an ad taken out by that same company," Davidson says. It's as good as a third-party testimonial.

The cost of getting an article about you or your business written and published, which may span several pages and include photos, is likely to be far less than the cost of a single-page ad in the same publication. While the advance planning, coordination, and acceptance of a self-generated article require some effort, it is often a sound investment. Even if targets don't see the article when it first runs, you can make attractive

**Los Angeles Times**

"Networking is far from peaking...[People] need to network to get business."

"Business Network Int'l... an organization that offers highly motivated business people a weekly no-nonsense breakfast meeting that virtually guarantees them customer leads."

**Arlington Morning News**

"The groups meet weekly for the sole purpose of networking and passing referrals to each other...BNI provides referrals in a more systematic way."

**THE DENVER POST**

"Word-of-Mouth is an impressive form of advertising because it suggests that recommendations come from people who are trusted and whose opinions are respected...Author Ivan Misner says, Word-of-Mouth marketing is a lot like farming, it's based on slow, nurturing care."

**Entrepreneur**

"A structured Word-of-Mouth marketing program that turns people into sales representatives for your company."

**THE TAMPA TRIBUNE**

"This is a way for people to give referrals to each other... a 15 member BNI chapter generates 45 to 50 monthly business referrals for members... With 30 members, the number triples."

"The members have worked like my own sales force to get business for me, Sheila Gardner...Members at BNI know they are there to work for one another and this commitment alone encourages referrals, added Susan Butler."

**The New York Times**

"We've had some tremendous stories. There is a printer in our group who met a real estate agent...That agency wanted to switch its printing and they gave him this job...It was more than a $100,000 job — and it happened because of a $200.00 investment."

**THE WALL STREET JOURNAL**

"With many small businesses scrambling to weather the recession, the networking business is thriving... Business people realize that in this tough economy they've got to do some extra things."

**The Boston Globe**

"In 1994, based on more than 300,000 referrals, BNI accounted for $105 million worth of new business [for its members]."

**THE INDIANAPOLIS STAR**

"Members of Indianapolis-area networking [groups] agree...It has been very good...members generated more than 304,000 referrals for each other. Those produced a little more than $106 million [for members], Misner said."

**Figure 7.2.** Excerpts from Articles on BNI in Major U.S. Newspapers and Magazines

reprints on high-quality, glossy stock and use them for several years as key items in your arsenal of collateral materials.

Surprisingly, editors and reporters need story ideas from wherever they can find them. Too many people who seek to be featured in newspapers or magazines send company brochures, or worse, capability statements. They fail to realize that editors and reporters need hooks, angles, ways to relate to a distracted, overworked, frenzied readership.

♦ *Getting an illustrated, multipage article written and published is likely to cost far less than a single-page ad in the same publication.*

Either by phone or by letter, tell the editor why readers will be interested in the feature idea you have, or why it is newsworthy. What are you doing in your business that strikes a chord in the community? What are the broad ramifications?

Be willing to become part of the story, not the story, and your odds of getting coverage will skyrocket.

Can you prime the pump with editors and reporters? Certainly. Read the publications you'd like to be in and find the reporter covering your beat. Then write or call with your best story idea. When you call, be as professional with the reporter or editor as you are with everyone else.

To locate all the newspapers and magazines in your area or across the country, visit the business reference section of your local library and ask to see *Bacon's Publicity Checker, Gebbie Press All-in-One Directory, Larriston's, Newspaper Rates and Data,* or *Working Press of the Nation.* In addition, you can get a very complete list on computer disk through the *Bates Directory* out of Lake Worth, Florida. With all these references, you'll have more than enough publication targets.

## Preparing Collateral Material

**I**f you already have news article reprints about yourself or your business, consider yourself ahead of the game. However, some of the other marketing materials you'll need for your word-of-mouth marketing effort include brochures and business cards (both with a well-designed logo) and other miscellaneous marketing materials. While a comprehensive discussion on preparing these materials exceeds the scope of this book, there are several books that offer considerable assistance, among them *The Copywriter's Handbook,* by Bob Bly; *Marketing on a Shoestring,* by Jeff Davidson; and *Great Promo Pieces,* by Herman Holtz.

Nearly every business needs literature that attractively conveys a message about how the company does business, what kinds of products and services it provides, and how to get in touch with it. Your referral partners can use well-designed collateral materials to send more business your way even faster. Here are a few tips.

## Brochures

A brochure is a handy and succinct way to market in print. If it is impressive enough, it may even be handed from one potential client to another. The best brochures have a fairly long "shelf life." They don't become outdated after a few months or even a year off the press, and they can be kept by clients as a reminder of your business.

Because of the multitude of purposes served by the brochure, you may need to spend more money on it than on other materials. The image created by your literature can make a strong impression on recipients. As a general rule, the look of your brochure needs to reflect what you want recipients to feel about your business, products, or services. The content of the brochure needs to specify what you want readers to know and understand about your business.

### Formula for an Excellent Brochure

- **Front cover.** The front cover of the brochure should include your business name (or the name of the products or services offered) and a brief, one-phrase or one-sentence description.

- **Inside.** Strive for completeness and conciseness in describing your business, products, or services. Immediately address who, what, where, when, and why.

- **A general "capabilities statement"** about what you can do and who can use your services.

- **Specific examples of achievements to date.** If your company is new, use examples of the kind of work you're prepared to do.

- **Quotes from satisfied clients and customers.** If you don't have any in writing, make some phone calls.

Remember, people want to know that you come highly recommended.

◆ **Price information,** if applicable.

◆ **Mail-in form or card.** Forms for placing orders, attending events, or requesting more information can help generate business.

◆ **Biographies of key personnel.** Use brief biographical sketches of the key people in your firm or those who will be directly providing the service offered.

◆ **Added attractions.** Mention any pluses briefly.

◆ **Name, address, phone number.** Display these prominently. Most recipients seek them on the back cover of the brochure.

Many associations already produce brochures members can use simply by adding a few customized lines giving their business name, address, and phone. This gives them an excellent opportunity to acquire quality literature and well-chosen content for a much smaller investment than they would need if they started from scratch.

## Logos

Logos leave a subtle but lasting impression. A good way to get started on developing a logo is to assemble the literature, business cards, and advertising pieces that you have on hand, spread them all out, and see what strikes your fancy. What design element makes an impact on you? Can you modify and improve on it, adapting it to your own product or service offering?

Another way to come up with a logo concept on your own is to develop a graphic logo using the name or initials of your business in a creative and eye-catching way. The letters can create their own design if presented in a way that makes them stand out.

## Business Cards

Business cards are an important part of your word-of-mouth campaign. Your card needs to show your company name, logo, address, telephone and fax numbers, along with your name and title.

If you are in a sales-related business, an attractive way to help others remember you is to use business cards with your photograph on them. Weeks and months after you've met, a person looking at your picture card feels in some sense more connected, more in touch with you. To that person, you become much more than a voice — you are an individual with an image. Although the picture business card costs more, for some professions the extra cost can easily pay for itself because of the better identification it provides.

## CHECKLIST OF MATERIALS

The box on the opposite page contains a quick checklist of items you may already have available or wish to begin assembling, that can be used as collateral materials in developing your desired image.

A parting word: To house such materials efficiently, purchase a bin or cubbyhole system, which is essentially a set of shelves built to make it easy to retrieve frequently used documents. Such units usually come with cubbyholes that are three or four across and twelve, eighteen, or twenty-four cubbyholes down. This equipment greatly aids any company's PR campaign and ability to respond quickly when necessary.

As part of the Hand-to-Hand WOMBAT Plan at the back of the book, you will find some worksheets to complete in order to take the first steps in creating a Positive Message, Delivered Effectively. Laying the foundation for building a word-of-mouth-based business includes creating a positive image that precedes you in the marketplace. By taking this approach, you enhance your credibility. Trust and credibility are prerequisites to getting people to refer you consistently.

## CHECKLIST OF COLLATERAL MATERIALS
## FOR DEVELOPING YOUR IMAGE

☐ Letters from satisfied customers

☐ Other collected comments, cards, messages from customers

☐ Photos of your office facilities, equipment, products (with staff, clients, etc.)

☐ Photos of your key customers' office facilities, equipment, products

☐ Photos of you and your staff

☐ Awards, certificates

☐ Articles in which you're mentioned

☐ Articles by you that have been published

☐ A one-page, *faxable* flyer

☐ Unpublished articles by you

☐ Audio or video cassettes you've used

☐ Any new-product announcements or press releases of yours that have been published

☐ Your Yellow Pages advertisement, if applicable

☐ Copies of other display advertisements that you've used

☐ Text from radio or TV advertisements that you've run

☐ A list of your memberships and affiliations

☐ Product catalogs you use

☐ Your existing brochures, circulars, or data sheets

☐ Question-and-answer sheets

☐ Logos, trademarks, service marks, patterns, designs you've used

☐ Your letterhead and stationery

☐ Your annual report, capability statement, prospectus

☐ Newsletters or news-type letters you use

☐ Your motto, mission statement, or service pledge

☐ Client or customer proposals and bid sheets

☐ Survey results by you or others

☐ Presentation notes, slides, or overheads

☐ Marketing letters you wrote to clients

☐ Generic materials developed by your association

☐ Articles on trends affecting your target niche

☐ Posters, banners, display materials used at trade shows

## HOT TIPS AND INSIGHTS

**1** A reassuring, professional image makes people feel more secure when buying something they can't see or hold in their hand, like a service.

**2** We are constantly bombarded with information and images through our daily work lives, travel, and television. We rightly or wrongly make snap judgments. So remember, the survival of your business is contingent upon how you position yourself and what you project.

**3** Positioning is an organized system for finding a window in the mind, recognizing that the most effective communication occurs when optimally placed and timed. Being first at something works well.

**4** Your success in business is often based on how you appear in print. An article is far more influential than an ad taken out by the same company.

**5** The cost of getting an article about you written and published, which may span several pages and include photos, is likely to be far less than that of a single-page ad in the same publication.

**6** Your referral partners can use well-designed collateral materials to send more business your way even faster.

**7** Because of the multitude of purposes and uses served by the brochure, you may need to spend more money on it than on many other materials. The look of your brochure needs to reflect what you want recipients to feel about your business, product, and/or services.

**8** Business cards are an important part of your word-of-mouth campaign. Your card needs to show your company name, logo, address, telephone and fax numbers, along with your name and title.

◆⁹ Use the bin system to quickly retrieve collateral materials and support your ongoing PR efforts.

◆¹⁰ A good public-relations campaign can substantially enhance your trust and credibility.

# Chapter 8

# Payoffs of Networking

## The Research Behind the Results

### NETWORKING AND WORD OF MOUTH

**T**hroughout history, people have made and used contacts to help them in their lives. People have always formed coalitions, because they know that sooner or later their welfare might depend on the willingness of others to help. While the practice of networking isn't new, its widespread use and sophistication have grown. During the late '70s and early '80s, the term "networking" came to mean a much more structured and sophisticated system of doing business.

Sometimes there is confusion between the terms "word of mouth" and "networking." Networking is part of the process you go through to build your word-of-mouth-based business. Through networking you can deliver your positive message effectively. Referrals are the end result.

Networking is the process of developing and using contacts to increase your business, enhance your knowledge, expand your sphere of influence, or serve the community. It is one of the most powerful techniques you can use to succeed in almost any venture. People network both formally and informally as a way of accomplishing these objectives. As I discuss networking throughout this book, keep in mind that it is networking for the express purpose of building a word-of-mouth-based business.

♦ *Through networking you can deliver your positive message effectively. Referrals are the end result.*

## WHAT NETWORKING IS NOT

**M**isconceptions about networking abound. I saw a newspaper editorial which implied that networkers were mercenaries who attacked a crowded room until no one was left untouched. According to the editorial, people who networked cared only about themselves and not those to whom they were speaking. The writer was basing her comments on several meetings where she had witnessed these so-called networkers in action.

There is a big difference, however, between good networking and bad networking, and what she undoubtedly saw was vivid examples of bad networking. It sounded to me as if some of the people she described had had a charisma bypass and that their major contribution to the event was to leave it. These people apparently were hawks who surrounded their quarry.

Implying that such people were typical of all networkers is a little like saying all salespeople are like Herb Tarlek, the salesman on the TV series *WKRP in Cincinnati*. Networking is as good or as bad as the person who happens to be doing it at that moment. The problem is that good networking is an acquired skill and one that not all people have acquired.

Until now, most people have been left on their own to develop their networking abilities. They have drawn upon management, sales, and social skills and then applied them to a loosely defined notion of networking. One of the reasons I wrote this book was to help you understand the skills and techniques required for becoming an effective or Notable Networker.

## NETWORKING VS. "NOTABLE NETWORKING"

**N**etworks are coalitions of business professionals who, through a mutual support system, help each other do more business. Notable Networking, when done right, is anything but superficial. On the contrary, it benefits all parties, not just one. If you want to build a word-of-mouth-based business, it must be based on the concept that givers gain; that is, if you want to get business, you have to give business to other business professionals. I believe the evidence to support this philosophy is overwhelming. People who are willing to give business will get business.

◆ *The key to building a word-of-mouth-based business is mutual support, relationship building, and the development of lasting professional friendships.*

With Notable Networking, many of the people with whom you network may be friends or become friends. The key to building a word-of-mouth-based business is mutual support, relationship building, and the development of lasting professional friendships. Members of a network are there to further their own business by helping each other. By meeting regularly, networks allow business people to get to know each other. It's through this exposure that people learn more about each other's businesses and feel comfortable about referring one another.

There is also a network that extends beyond the members of a networking organization. Each member of a network knows dozens of people who, in turn, know dozens of others, and so on. As such, a group of thirty to forty may know thousands of other people throughout the business community. Thus, networks often have a greater impact than their size may initially indicate. This is especially true in tight-knit groups that meet regularly and track the quantity and quality of referrals given.

## YOUR FREE SALES FORCE

Organizations that network well provide opportunities for developing and exchanging quality business referrals. Hence, being a member of a well-organized network is like having dozens of salespeople working for you, each referring prospective clients your way. No, these referrals aren't guaranteed sales. However, they typically are serious prospective clients. When this extended network is functioning properly, it will bring you most of your business referrals.

Many unsuccessful business people hang out a shingle, buy some ads, and wait for business to come streaming in. But successful business people work hard at increasing their business by developing referrals.

## PROVEN RESULTS

Having spent most of the last two decades participating in or managing business development networks across the country, I have amassed substantial evidence suggesting that such organizations are among the most effective means of generating word-of-mouth business.

A study done by Robert Davis at the University of San Francisco, for example, found that people participating in networking groups "appear to be above-average networkers." The study concludes that participants in networking groups develop certain networking skills that the average business professional does not possess, and that these skills in fact result in more referrals to other business professionals, leading to substantially more new clients. This makes a very strong argument for participating in organized networking groups.

> ◆ *Business development networks are among the most effective means of generating word-of-mouth business.*

As part of my doctoral work at the University of Southern California, I conducted a thorough study of referral generation amongst members of BNI. In the study I found that the longer an individual participates in a business development network, the greater the number of referrals. In fact, the likelihood of receiving a hundred or more referrals virtually doubles with each passing year of participation. One participant told me that in his first year as a member he received roughly $6,000 in referrals for his paging business. During his second year, he got over $11,000, and in his third year more than $22,000! The study clearly showed that the longer people participated in their networking group, the higher the return.

## TIME EQUALS MONEY

S ome of the most exciting discoveries from my doctoral study involve length of membership in a networking group. For example, the study found that the people who were members for one to two years identified their largest referral to be over fifty times higher than people who had been members for less than one year!

| Years of Membership: | 0-1 | 1-2 | 2-3 | 3-4 | 4+ |
|---|---|---|---|---|---|
| Largest single referral (net income): | | | | | |
| Under $1,000 | 76.3 | 57.5 | 40.9 | 27.0 | 20.0 |
| Over $1,000 | 23.7 | 42.5 | 59.1 | 73.0 | 80.0 |
| | | (percent by category) | | | |

**Figure 8.1.** Impact of Length of Membership on Large Referrals

This trend continues as long as the person remains a member. For example, 52.3 percent of the respondents who were members for less than a year stated that their largest referral was $250 or less, while only 7.5 percent said it was over $2,500. On the other hand, none of the respondents who were members for several years said that their largest referral was under $250, while 52 percent said their largest referral was over $2,500, with 32 percent actually exceeding $5,000! Thus, large referrals are directly related to length of membership. In other words, individuals who stay with a networking group longer are much more likely to get referrals that are substantially larger.

Figure 8.1 illustrates this point. You will note that the longer someone was a member, the higher the likelihood he or she would receive a referral worth over $1,000. It should be noted that many of these referrals were *substantially* over $1,000 (in some cases over $100,000). In some years many members got at least one referral worth more than $10,000 in business.

It is clear that the longer an individual is a member of a business development network, the greater the individual's opportunity to get larger referrals. In fact, members are almost twice as likely to get referrals worth over $1,000 in net income if they are in the group for more than one year. In addition, the overall number of referrals increases substantially the longer someone participates, as shown in figure 8.2.

| Years of Membership: | 0–1 | 1–2 | 2–3 | 3–4 | 4+ |
|---|---|---|---|---|---|
| Number of referrals: | | | | | |
| 0–9 | 57.4 | 13.5 | 9.9 | 0.0 | 0.0 |
| 10–19 | 23.1 | 24.5 | 8.5 | 8.1 | 16.0 |
| 20–29 | 10.1 | 16.8 | 19.7 | 10.8 | 8.0 |
| 30–39 | 3.4 | 17.4 | 14.1 | 16.2 | 4.0 |
| 40–49 | 2.7 | 5.8 | 8.5 | 13.5 | 4.0 |
| 50–59 | 1.9 | 11.6 | 21.1 | 18.9 | 4.0 |
| 60–99 | 1.1 | 7.7 | 12.7 | 21.6 | 40.0 |
| 100+ | 0.4 | 2.6 | 5.6 | 10.8 | 24.0 |

(percent by category)

Figure 8.2. Number of Referrals by Years of Membership

## SPIN-OFF REFERRALS

A nother interesting finding from this study was that the longer an individual participated in the group, the greater the percentage of "spin-off" (referrals from referrals) business he or she could expect. Comments from the respondents regarding spin-off referrals were numerous and consistent. Most explained the conditions under which they received or closed spin-off referrals. For example, a photographer who was a member of his group for almost two years received a referral to a service company from another member. The company had him take photographs of all sixty employees. These led to individual requests for family portraits and eventually the company's annual awards banquet. That one referral was worth almost $10,000 in spin-off business alone.

A painting contractor told of a real-estate agent in his chapter who had listed a home that needed exterior painting in order to sell. He was hired to do the job. He stated that while he was painting the home, "The neighbors decided they wanted me to paint the exterior to their home also." The new client had a friend around the block who wanted some interior and exterior painting done; the contractor was hired for that job as well. In the meantime, the original client sold his home; the new owners decided to redecorate and needed a complete new interior paint job. According to the contractor, "When everything was finished, that one original referral added up to well over $11,000 worth of spin-off business."

## WORD OF MOUTH WORKS ANYWHERE

**A**nother interesting fact relates to different areas of the country. An unpublished part of the study found that there was no statistically significant difference between parts of the country regarding either the amount of new business generated by a member or the average value of a referral to that member. This means that the part of the country (East Coast, West Coast, Midwest, North, South, etc.) plays no part in the amount of business that someone might expect to get by participating in a Strong Contact Network. This is important, because I often hear people tell me, "That won't work in this city; we don't do things that way here." Well, the evidence shows that people who are successful at word-of-mouth marketing create their referral business basically the same way everywhere, regardless of the weather, the time zones, the population, or the attitudes of the area.

What I have learned over the years is that people, like water, tend to seek the path of least resistance. That is, they will sometimes attempt to do what is easiest rather than what is most effective. The most incredible thing of all is that they will then blame it on the area they live in. This is particularly true if they can point to some cultural straw-man argument like "People in this area don't like to get up early for business meetings." Hello, excuse me, many people *everywhere* don't particularly like to get up early for meetings. But they will, if they want to be successful at building their business. Don't let the naysayers convince you that you can't do what other people are doing very successfully. I've seen too many people make excuses for not doing something because they have it in their head that "that's just not done here." On the other hand, I've seen tens of thousands of business people from all over the world who have successfully built their businesses using the concepts I am discussing in this book. This really shouldn't be surprising, because if a concept works, it should work pretty much everywhere business people are looking to increase their income.

| Gender: | Male | Female |
|---|---|---|
| Number of referrals: | | |
| 0–9 | 40.0 | 38.5 |
| 10–19 | 18.7 | 24.7 |
| 20–29 | 14.3 | 9.2 |
| 30–39 | 7.4 | 8.6 |
| 40–49 | 4.8 | 3.9 |
| 50–59 | 6.5 | 6.6 |
| 60–99 | 5.7 | 5.9 |
| 100+ | 2.6 | 2.6 |
| | (% by category) | |

**Figure 8.3.** Number of Referrals by Gender of Member

## GENDER NOT A FACTOR

The study also found that women were well represented and did as much business as the men (fig. 8.3). Although men and women received and closed the same amount of business, it had, according to the women, a higher impact on them.

A female CPA stated, "I am reasonably new in business. Since I became a member of the organization more than a year ago, 66 percent of my billings have been a result of my membership, some of them second-generation referrals. In total, over 37 percent of my billings have been a direct result of the word-of-mouth sales force represented by this group."

## THE NEXT STEP

This chapter has attempted to show clear evidence that word-of-mouth marketing, when done right, works very well. Networking is an integral element of that process because it helps you deliver a positive message effectively. Studies show that people involved in structured networking programs are above average at generating and receiving referrals. Furthermore, evidence indicates that the longer people are active in business groups, the larger the referrals they receive. Gender does not appear to be a factor: both men and women benefit from this approach.

A structured word-of-mouth marketing program works well because it incorporates the aid of people who, along with you, are looking to increase their business through referrals. Good intentions are not enough, however. In the next chapter, I will outline some of the important skills that I think are necessary in order to deliver your message effectively. These skills or "laws" are the cornerstone of the effective application of your word-of-mouth marketing program.

## HOT TIPS AND INSIGHTS

❶ Networking is part of the process you go through to build your word-of-mouth-based business. Through networking you can deliver your positive message effectively. Referrals are the end result.

❷ The key to building a word-of-mouth-based business is mutual support, relationship building, and the development of lasting professional friendships.

❸ Being a member of a well-organized network is like having dozens of salespeople working for you, each referring prospective clients your way.

❹ People who participate in networking groups are above-average networkers.

❺ The longer people participate in a network, the greater the average number of referrals they receive.

### Chapter 9

# Three Laws of Notable Networking

## *The Secrets to Delivering Your Message Effectively*

### THE THREE LAWS OF NOTABLE NETWORKING

**O**ver the last ten years, I've met individuals who have developed such incredible networking skills that they get almost 100 percent of their business through referrals. They've been successful at building a word-of-mouth-based business because they're as committed to giving referrals as they are to following up on the referrals they get. What does it take to achieve results like these?

There are three requirements or laws for becoming a Notable (or effective) Networker. Without applying these laws, you would find it impossible to work your networks effectively.

At face value the laws seem simple, but don't let first impressions deceive you. Behind these simple-sounding principles lies a comprehensive set of requirements and obligations. If you don't heed these laws, you will invest many hours and some dollars into networking groups but get a poor return on your investment.

## THE FIRST LAW OF NOTABLE NETWORKING: HAVE A POSITIVE AND SUPPORTIVE ATTITUDE

**G**ood networking involves providing a positive and supportive environment to other business people. If you retain nothing else you read in this book, remember this: Notable Networking is predicated upon the concept that givers gain.

If you freely give business to others, they will give business to you. This concept is based on the age-old notion that "what goes around, comes around." If I give business to you, you'll give business to me, and we will both do better as a result.

♦ *Notable Networking is predicated upon the concept that givers gain.*

Networking is like a savings account: if you keep investing wisely, you can draw upon it when you need it. One enthusiastic networker who belongs to a formal networking group told me, "The longer I'm in the group, the better I get at networking and the more referrals I get. In addition, it seems that the more referrals I get, the higher the percentage that I close! By developing long-term relationships, I am gaining the trust of the other members, which makes it easier to receive and close the referrals that are passed to me."

A positive, supportive attitude also includes the way you present yourself to other people. Everyone likes to do business with an enthusiastic optimist. If you join a networking group, remain focused on the reason you're there. I see far too many people go to networks and get caught up in irrelevant nitpicking: "The food's no good," "The speaker was mediocre," "This room's not very nice," and so on.

♦ *The First Law of Notable Networking is more than an attitude: it's a way of life and a good way to do business.*

With the quibblers, I share this anecdote: An airline attendant once responded to a passenger's complaints about the quality of his dinner by asking him, "When you go to a French restaurant, do you usually order an airline ticket?" The same rationale applies to networking meetings. The quality of the food and the speaker should be *secondary* to the quality of the contacts you are making. Don't lose sight of your purpose.

It's not Net-Sit or Net-Eat, it's Net-WORK! If you want your network to work for you, then you have to work your network in a positive and supportive manner.

In many ways, the First Law of Notable Networking involves more than attitude; it's a way of life and a good way to do business. When you constantly and consciously keep other people in mind, they will do the same for you.

## THE SECOND LAW OF NOTABLE NETWORKING: LEARN HOW TO USE NETWORKING TOOLS EFFECTIVELY

A Notable Networker must have and use the right tools to network skillfully. All professionals need the tools of their trade to conduct business. A painter needs a brush, a teacher needs a blackboard, and a secretary needs a computer.

To achieve success, networkers need their own tools as well. Good networkers' tools include

- name tags to identify themselves to others,
- card holders to carry their business cards, and most important,
- card files to carry other people's business cards.

It has been said that the U.S. Chamber of Commerce coined the term "networking." Over the years, I've gone to many Chamber of Commerce business mixers. Unfortunately, too many of them seem to practice a passive form of the technique. However, depending on the chamber, some mixers can be an outstanding way to meet many new people. At Chamber of Commerce mixers, people from a variety of businesses get together with the idea of meeting one another.

*◆ I can't imagine going to a business meeting and not telling everyone what business I'm in!*

At these meetings, I often encounter people who don't wear a name tag. Of those who do, many neglect to put their company name or profession on the badge. I can't imagine anyone going to a business meeting and not telling everyone what business he or she is in! You've got to let people know who you are and what business you're in if you want to reap the full rewards of networking.

I also run into people who don't have any business cards with them. Business cards are one of the most inexpensive forms of advertising available and a crucial tool for networking. They should be well designed and present a professional image. Most important, you need to have them in your possession! A large stack of cards sitting in the desk drawer at your office doesn't help much at a business mixer. Always carry a small metal card case full of business cards with you and keep a large box of business cards in the glove compartment or trunk of your car for restocking your card case on the spot. Use the backs of any cards you get from others to make notes that will jog your memory about each individual or about the conversation you had.

In addition, you should go a step further and carry a vinyl or leather card-carrying case or book (like those produced by the Hazel company) for the cards of people you network with. These are people in your own personal network of contacts, people who presumably are storing your cards and referring you as well. Always keep three or four of their cards so you can hand one to anyone interested in their services.

One way to enhance your networking efforts is to use computer software. When you get back to your office, you can enter the new names and information you've acquired into a contact management program. Such programs as Outlook 98, Act, and Goldmine help you organize your information and enable you to easily handle follow-up activities. In addition to these, several general database programs, such as Access, provide some contact management capabilities. Each has its own direction, but all of them cover the essentials. You log in new information and contacts, and upon command you get reports of your progress and reminders as to who needs to be called back. If you're not already using these programs and enthralled by what they do for you, relax — the learning time is a couple of hours or less. If that's too long for you, take a look at the latest business-card scanners, which allow you to run a business card through them and log all the necessary information directly into your database. Now if only they could go to the meetings for you, too.

## THE THIRD LAW OF NOTABLE NETWORKING: NETWORKING IS AN ACQUIRED SKILL

Most people are not born networkers; they develop the skills through education, training, the right attitude, and long practice. Any technique of value requires a commitment to learning how to use it effectively. The next generation of business professionals will operate under a different model of management, in which networking will be an integral element. Take advantage of every opportunity you have to learn to network more effectively. It is a skill that will only grow in importance.

Remember Will Rogers's statement about being on the right track: "If you're just sitting there, you're going to get run over!" If you are active in a networking organization, you're "on the right track." The key, however, is to take advantage of the opportunities that these groups have to offer. This means you need to be an active participant in the networking process to get any substantive results.

Curiously, many people invest time in networking, but not in learning how. This is like trying to play tennis or golf without lessons. Sure, you can perform, but how well? Simply attending meetings is not enough. You need to listen to tapes, read books and articles, talk to people who network well, and most important, practice what you've learned. This is no less than what you would do to learn how to play golf, manage people, or sell a product.

Your next step on the road to developing a word-of-mouth-based business is to attend every networking event that you can and *practice, practice, practice!* Practice greeting people, handing out your card, asking for their cards, listening, excusing yourself, and introducing yourself to others. There are many skills to acquire and to perfect; you can't expect to become a master after your first couple of visits to various networking functions. *Delivering a positive message* means that you must know and apply the techniques I've talked about in this chapter. Review the Hand-to-Hand WOMBAT Plan at the end of this book to incorporate some of the key elements of this section into your own personalized word-of-mouth campaign.

## HOT TIPS AND INSIGHTS

❶ Notable Networkers are people who are skilled at networking and committed to the idea that givers gain; by helping other businesses get new clients or customers, they get new business sent their way.

**2** The key to building a word-of-mouth-based business is mutual support, not necessarily friendship.

**3** Organizations that network effectively provide opportunities to develop and exchange quality business referrals. Being a member of a well-organized network is like having dozens of salespeople working for you, each referring prospective clients your way.

**4** A Notable Networker must have a positive and supportive attitude. Good networking involves providing a positive and supportive environment for other business people.

**5** A Notable Networker must have and use the right tools to network skillfully, including an informative name badge, business cards, and business-card carrying case to hold others' cards.

**6** Networking is an acquired skill; it requires listening to tapes, reading books and articles, talking to people who network well, and practicing what you've learned.

**7** Effective networking requires practice, practice, and then more practice.

### Chapter 10

# Rewarding Referrals

## Getting People to Send You Business

## CREATIVITY WORKS

**Y**ou can greatly enhance your word-of-mouth-based business by designing creative incentives for people to give you referrals. Yet of all the key techniques for making the system work, this one seems to frustrate people the most.

Historically, finder's fees have been used as an incentive for giving someone referrals. Although finder's fees can be appropriate,

I don't believe they are necessarily the best technique to employ in most situations. Here is an excellent example of a nonmonetary incentive system:

Years ago I went to my chiropractor for a routine adjustment. Several weeks before, I had referred a friend to him who had recently been in an accident. As I walked into the waiting room, I noticed a bulletin board that was displayed prominently on the wall. The bulletin board read, "We would like to thank the following patients for referring someone to us last month."

Actually, there was nothing unusual about this sign. It had been there on each of my previous visits, except this time my name was posted on it. I took notice and was pleased, but didn't give it a second thought, until a month later, when I returned and saw that my name was no longer on it. Instantly I thought, Who else can I refer to the doctor so that my name will be put back on the board? For the record, I did come up with another referral for the good doctor.

Something like this may not work for everyone. But if it worked on me, I'm sure it will have a positive affect on others. The key is to select several incentive options so as to impact as many people as possible.

## THE IMPORTANCE OF INCENTIVES

An incentive in this context is anything that gets people to refer you to others. Many doctors' offices use the technique listed above. It works well for at least two reasons:

1. The bulletin board is a continual reminder to patients that the office wants their referrals.
2. People like to be recognized for their efforts.

Some health care professionals offer a free visit when a referral becomes a new patient. Other business professionals send small gift baskets, bottles of wine, flowers, or certificates for their services or the services of other businesses in the community. Depending on the type of product or service you offer and the relationship with your referring parties, you may also employ

- ◆ Free estimates, samples, or analyses
- ◆ Additional products or services for no extra cost
- ◆ Product or service discounts
- ◆ Product or service time extensions
- ◆ Extended telephone consultation privileges
- ◆ Extended or life memberships
- ◆ Exclusive or charter memberships
- ◆ Group discounts
- ◆ Extended warranties
- ◆ Reduced costs on peripheral items or services

One enterprising entrepreneur developed a program whereby an existing customer would receive a $500 bonus coupon toward a purchase on his next order for referring a new customer. In this case, each new customer represented several thousands of dollars worth of business, so the $500 bonus coupon was a bargain.

When you offer any type of discount or novelty item as an incentive for referrals, keep in mind what your cost would be to generate a new client or customer from scratch, including the cost of printed literature, advertisements, sales calls, telephone time, meetings, appointments, and so forth. You can readily see that the cost of gaining a new client through a referral incentive program is almost always lower.

Incentive programs also help you sell more products or services more frequently to your existing customer base; again, these are sales that are generated at a far lower marketing cost and effort.

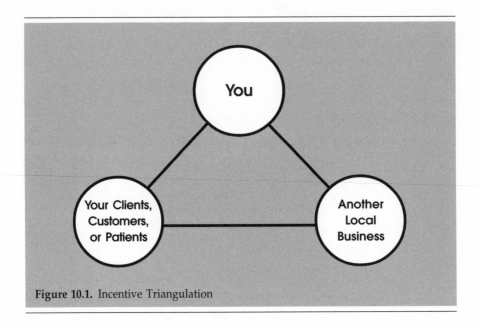

**Figure 10.1.** Incentive Triangulation

## INCENTIVE TRIANGULATION

**S**ome resourceful business people use a technique that I call "Incentive Triangulation" (fig. 10.1). This is a powerful way of leveraging other people's services to benefit your customers, clients, or patients. The concept is simple and can be designed to fit the needs or requirements of any business. For example, a retailer might negotiate an arrangement with another local business, such as a florist, printer, or appliance store owner, whereby that store will provide their customers with a discount of 10 percent or more on their next purchase. Thereafter, each time someone gives you a referral, reward him or her with whatever you would normally give as an incentive and also a coupon good for the discount at the prearranged business.

This form of joint venture is beneficial for all three parties, hence the term "Incentive Triangulation." You benefit because you are providing another incentive for people to refer you. The other business benefits because you are sending your clients to it, along with a recommendation, of course. Finally, your clients benefit because they get recognition for their effort as well as an additional product or service at a reduced rate. Granted, this type of incentive may not be appropriate for all professions. Where appropriate, however, it works very well.

## Finding the Right Incentive Program

**N**o matter what form of incentive program you use, the fact that you offer incentives means that your potential for generating word-of-mouth business will increase. The question is, what type of incentive will work for you?

To meet the challenge of finding the right incentive program, tap into the assistance and insights of other people. An effective way to do this is to invite about ten people you know to meet with you. Include a representative sample of your customers/clients/patients, business associates, partners, and friends. Their purpose is to think up incentives you could offer to produce a larger word-of-mouth-based business. Host a lunch or dinner for the group and either take copious notes or tape-record the meeting. Invite those who are willing to donate about two hours for your benefit (and receive a free meal, of course).

Prepare yourself, well in advance of the group meeting. Think the subject over beforehand so you have an idea of the limits that you may need to set for an incentive program, such as cost, duration, appropriateness, etc. Have soft drinks, note pads, a preliminary questionnaire, sample materials, a flip chart, and even a few ideas to get the ball rolling. If you're going to discuss a product, bring actual samples to give the group a point of reference.

Begin the actual session by clearly stating a specific problem. Make sure your group understands that the incentive has to be geared to the group you've targeted. Explain that you are looking for a variety of ideas and that you won't make any immediate decisions.

## BRAINSTORMING

T he concept of brainstorming was originated by Alex F. Osborn to help trigger creative ideas in advertising. Following the meal, you or a designated party leads a brainstorming session to generate ideas on an effective incentive program for your business. For maximum creativity, four basic principles must be fully understood and followed, according to Osborn:

**1. Judicial judgment is ruled out.** Criticism of ideas must be withheld until later; otherwise you run the risk of shutting down the idea pipeline. The first time I used brainstorming, we tried to evaluate each idea as it came up, and the entire session went way too long.

**2. "Freewheeling" is welcome.** The wilder the idea, the better; it's easier to tame down ideas than to think them up. Moreover, wild ideas often lead to creative solutions. I've found that the way an idea is first presented by someone doesn't always register with others. With a twist and turn, however, ideas seemingly from Mars are brought back to Earth and become eminently workable.

**3. Quantity is desirable.** The greater the number of ideas, the better the likelihood of winners. Don't be afraid if you have to go to the second or third page of a flip chart. You want at least twelve ideas so you'll have plenty to work with once everyone runs out of steam.

**4. Combination and improvement are also desirable.** In addition to contributing ideas of their own, participants should suggest how ideas of others can be turned into better ideas, or how two or more ideas can be joined into still another idea. Some ideas that aren't workable alone become quite effective in combination.

Once you've exhausted all the ideas for possible incentives, review the list item by item and try to narrow it down to a manageable number. Don't worry about how you're going to do something until you've determined all the options. After most of the ideas are exhausted, spend time discussing those that are left and get feedback on which ones may be most effective. Last, select the idea or ideas that you'll put into practice.

The process we've just reviewed is known as the "focus-group technique." Such groups have been used in market research for many years and are excellent for gathering data as well as probing attitudes on many marketing-related subjects.

At the end of the session, if the sparks were really flying, suggest that the group meet again soon. As such, it could evolve from a one- or two-time focus group into your own advisory board. Even if you meet quarterly or semiannually, there is still great value in having reconvened to discuss the challenges you're working on.

## CREATIVE INCENTIVES

C reativity is the key to any good incentive program. People just naturally like to help each other, but especially when they know their efforts are successful. Let your contact know when a referral he or she has made comes through, and be as creative as you can.

I've heard many novel ways business people reward those who send them referrals. A female consultant sends bouquets of flowers to men. A music store owner sends concert tickets. A financial planner sends change purses and money clips.

An accountant in St. Louis thanks those who successfully refer a client to him by paying for a dinner for two at an exclusive restaurant at least one hour's drive from their homes. This approach firmly plants the accountant in the minds of his referral sources: they won't be able to use it right away because the distance requires that they plan for it. As the date approaches, because it has been planned, they'll be talking about it, and probably about the accountant. Later, when the referring party runs into someone else who might need an accountant, who will he recommend?

One Realtor I met in Northern California told me that for almost six years he had offered a one-hundred-dollar finder's fee to anyone giving him a referral that led to a listing or sale. He said that in all that time he had given only about a dozen finder's fees, so he decided to try another kind of incentive.

Living on a large parcel of land in prime wine country, he had begun growing grapes in his own vineyard. A thought occurred to him: Why not take the next step? He began processing the grapes and bottling his own special vintage wine. After his first harvest, he had a graphic artist design a beautiful label, which he affixed to each bottle. He told all his friends that he did not sell this wine; he gave it as a gift to anyone providing him with a bona fide referral.

He gave away dozens of cases in the first three years — half the time it took him to give only one dozen cash finder's fees. Yet each bottle cost him less than ten dollars to produce. This special vintage wine makes him infinitely more money than giving away a handful of hundred-dollar finder's fees.

About two weeks after the first edition of this book went to the printer, I got a call from the Realtor. "Has your book gone into print?" he asked. I told him it had. "Too bad," he replied. "I've got a terrific story for you.

"Last Friday I got a phone call from a woman I didn't know. Out of the blue, she gave me two referrals. As I wrote down the information, I asked her how she had heard of me.

"She said, 'I had dinner last night at a friend's house. He served wine. I took a sip. "Wow, great wine!" I told him. "Where did you buy it?" "You can't buy it," he said. "The only way you can get it is to give this real estate agent a referral."

"'I have two referrals,' she said. 'Can I get two bottles?'

"So I gladly sent her two bottles. Both referrals turned into business, and each of them cost me only ten dollars."

It sometimes amazes me, even now, how something as simple as a bottle of wine can be such a powerful incentive for people to give you referrals. But the explanation is really quite simple: because it's special. A bottle of wine that can't be bought can be worth ten times what it cost to produce when traded for something as valuable as a business referral.

## INCENTIVES FOR THOSE AROUND YOU

**A**re there employees, co-workers, friends, or relatives who might be able to refer you? It always surprises me that people forget to provide incentives for the individuals working with them. You'll probably need to offer different kinds of incentives for different groups of people. You may choose to offer something completely different for your employees than you would for your clients or networking associates, such as bonuses and vacation days.

Remember, finding the right incentive is considered the biggest challenge by most individuals who are preparing to score big by building word-of-mouth business. To make it easier on yourself, be sure to get opinions and feedback from others who have a significant interest in your success.

Take a few minutes to review the Hand-to-Hand WOMBAT Plan in the back of the book to prepare your own personal incentive program. Don't underestimate the value of recognizing the people who send you business. A well-thought-out incentive program will add much to your word-of-mouth program.

### HOT TIPS AND INSIGHTS

**1** An incentive is anything that gets people to refer you to others. Creative incentives work best.

**2** Your word-of-mouth-based business can be greatly enhanced if you design some creative incentives for people to give you referrals. Of all the key techniques for making the system work, this one seems to frustrate people the most.

**3** Although finder's fees can be appropriate, they are not the best ploy to use in most situations.

**4** Depending on the type of product or service you offer, you may employ as incentives free estimates, samples, or analyses, additional products or services for no extra cost, product or service discounts, product or service time extensions, extended telephone consultation privileges, extended memberships, life memberships, exclusive or charter memberships, group discounts, extended warranties, or reduced costs on peripheral items or services.

**5** Incentive Triangulation benefits you by providing an incentive for another business to refer you. The other business benefits because you are sending your clients to it along with a recommendation. Your clients benefit because they get recognition for their effort, as well as an additional product or service at a reduced rate.

**6** To find the right incentive program, tap the assistance and insights of other people through a focus group.

**7** Lead your focus group in a brainstorming session to generate ideas for an effective incentive program for your business. Avoid criticizing any ideas, welcome freewheeling, seek many ideas, and piggyback on the ideas presented.

### Chapter 11

# **M**aking Introductions That Last

*Creating Your Memory Hooks*

## PERSONAL INTRODUCTIONS

**Y**our primary goal in building a word-of-mouth-based business is to increase the amount of business you get. To do this, you must make meaningful contact with other business professionals who can either use your services, refer someone else who can use your services, or both. Thus, word-of-mouth marketing is a team sport.

One of the fundamental elements of this process is making effective introductions. The ideal introduction is brief and memorable — one that provides enough impact to arouse the interest of those to whom you're introducing yourself and get them to join your word-of-mouth "team."

Think of networking as a relay race. Your personal introduction serves the same purpose as passing the baton from one runner to the next. Because you have to reach out and pass the baton to the next runner and he in turn has to reach back and receive it, the baton pass is a cooperative activity.

When planning your personal introduction, your goal is to deliver information another person or a group would be interested in hearing and to recognize that they may be interested in giving you some information about themselves to pass to another runner. In theory, there is no limit to the number of runners or the distance covered in your relay race.

The baton exchange takes place in an instant; there's no time or chance for a second attempt. If the baton is not placed in the open hand of the next runner, it will fall to the ground. Personal introductions can suffer the same fate. A poorly planned personal introduction can fall on deaf ears. It won't be passed on.

## STAND AND DELIVER

W hether you're introducing yourself to an individual or to a group, you have a choice of how you deliver your message. The primary vehicle for your introduction is your verbal presentation. Does your introduction work?

People will judge not only the message, but the messenger as well. How you look, carry yourself, listen, and leave the conversation will affect what others do with the message you've delivered. The important thing to remember is to speak as if you're addressing a single person, a good friend.

As you network with friends and associates and tell them what you do, your underlying hope is that they will use your services and pass the message to others, who will also use your services and in turn keep spreading your message. When someone such as a Strong or Casual Contact speaks on your behalf, the same rules apply. What you do and say sets the pattern for duplication. As in the "telephone game" you may have played as a child, you need to keep checking down the line to ensure that your original message is being accurately passed along. As you continue to build your word-of-mouth network, you need to know how much information your fellow networkers are actually hearing and understanding. Hence, you'll probably need to make some adjustments in the way you disseminate your message.

Each messenger may have used a different technique and had different motives for participating in the race, but the essence of each message is what needs to cross the finish line.

## NO TIME FOR SMALL TALK

S erious networkers, recognizing that they have limited time to introduce themselves and convey the essence of what they do, generally avoid *lengthy* small talk.

If you want to build your business through word of mouth, you must give a message that's heard by others. Take the time to plan your introduction and prepare some concise and descriptive overviews of your products or services. Then, when you meet someone for the first time, you can give him a good explanation of what you have to offer. I recommend that you develop several scripts that you can readily use when attending networking meetings.

Show pride in who you are and what you do. When Martha Taft was a young girl in elementary school, she was asked to introduce herself to a group of people. "My name is Martha Bowers Taft," said the child. "My great-grandfather was President of the United States. My grandfather was a United States Senator. My daddy is Ambassador to Ireland. And I am a Brownie."

## BRIEF INTRODUCTIONS

**W**hen participating, even as a guest, in various business organizations, you will be required to introduce yourself. Preparing a script for introducing yourself will improve your results. One of your scripts should be an overview of what you do. Other presentations can address various aspects of your product or service. Here's the recommended sequence for a script:

- ◆ Your name
- ◆ Your business or profession
- ◆ A brief description of your business or profession
- ◆ A Memory Hook (a short, ear-catching phrase)
- ◆ A benefit statement of one of your products or services (what you do that helps others)
- ◆ Your name, again

Your name and your business or profession are easy enough. A brief description, Memory Hook, and benefit statement can be separate items, but more often they are intertwined in your message. For example, it's easy to combine your business with the benefits of your product or service. I suggest telling people what you do, as well as what you are:

*◆ In organizations where all the members introduce themselves at each meeting, it is vitally important to vary your presentations.*

"I'm a financial planner, and I help people plan for their future."

"I'm an advertising and marketing consultant; I help companies get the most out of their advertising dollar."

These explanations are more effective than saying, "I do financial planning," or "I plan advertising campaigns."

In many situations, you'll be introducing yourself to only one or two people at a time. Some networking organizations have all the members stand at each meeting, and in round-robin fashion, give a one-minute overview to the entire group. If you're a member of a group like this, it is vitally important to vary your presentations.

Many people who are in business groups that meet every week have a tendency to say the same old thing, time after time. From what I've seen, many *weekly* presentations are done *weakly*. If you do this, many people will tune you out when you speak, because they've already heard your message several times. Your best bet is to give a brief overview, then concentrate on just one element of your business for the rest of your presentation.

## MEMORY HOOKS

Memory Hooks are excellent tools to use when making a presentation. A Memory Hook is something in your presentation that so vividly describes what you do that people will be able to visualize it clearly in their mind's eye. This visualization of your product or service makes it easier for them to refer you whenever they meet someone who needs your service.

For example, I met an interconnect (telephone) sales representative at a meeting of BNI. When his turn came to give his sixty-second commercial, he painted a vivid picture in everyone's mind about the type of company that needed his product: He said, "The next time you're in someone's office, look at their telephone system. If they have a phone system with fat wires, they need me."

He explained that old phone systems use thick wires while new, more advanced systems use thin wires. Consequently, anyone with fat wires has an old, inefficient phone system, and he could offer that person a more cost-effective alternative. To this day, every time I go into someone's office I look under the secretary's desk to see if the phone system has fat wires! (I've had more than one secretary say to me, "Dr. Misner, is there something I can help you with? Is there something you're looking for under my desk?" How do you explain to a secretary that you're just looking for fat wires under her desk?) It's been almost ten years, yet I still remember that Memory Hook as though it were yesterday. The result is that this salesman, in effect, has many "salespeople" like me out in the business community looking for businesses who need his service.

A good Memory Hook doesn't have to be funny, but it helps. A skin care consultant once rose at a meeting I was attending and said, "If you have a face, you could use my products. If you know someone who has a face, they could use my products." A lot of people remembered her because of her humor in describing her target market. She went on to explain to everyone that her products were not just for women, but for men, women, and children — anyone with a face.

> ♦ *A good Memory Hook doesn't have to be funny, but it helps.*

A security-systems consultant stood up at a networking meeting to give his sixty-second commercial, paused for a few seconds for dramatic effect, and proclaimed, "I have a criminal mind! If you use me, I'll try to break into your house. By doing so, I'll be able to show you how a real criminal can get into your house in a matter of minutes. But more important, I'll be able to show you how to stop him!" What a great presentation! I looked around the room and saw everyone giving complete attention. He had successfully used dramatic flair to create an excellent Memory Hook.

At a different meeting, a rotund fellow who owned a popular Italian restaurant stood up. While holding his belly out for all to view he exclaimed, "As you can see, I'm a walking billboard for our pasta!" He proceeded to describe in mouthwatering detail how his restaurant used only the finest cheeses, handmade pasta, and a wonderful slow-cooked sauce made from the freshest ingredients. By the time he was finished, all the people in the room were ready to finish their networking in his restaurant.

One gentlemen stunned his group by saying, "Did you ever want to shoot a relative? Call me, I'm a photographer!"

Here are some other notable Memory Hooks I've had the privilege of being hooked with over the years:

- Carpet cleaner: "We steal dirt from houses."

- Chiropractor: "You'll feel fine when your spine's in line." Or, "We're always glad to see you're back."

- Dentist: "We cater to cowards." Or, "My filling station is downtown, where I put the bite on decay."

- Electrical contractor: "For your commercial and residential electrical needs . . . give us a call and we'll check out your shorts."

- Fitness instructor: "If you wear out your body, where are you going to live?"

- Hairdresser: "If your hair is not becoming to you, then you should be coming to me."

- Insurance: "If you drive it, live in it, or work at it, we can insure it!"

- Lawyer: "Before you turn to dust, see me for your will or trust."

- Maternity-shop owner: "We carry everything for you but the baby."

- Plumber: "Remember, a flush is always better than a full house."

- Realtor: "I help people find a home — not a house, but a home. Not a place where you live, but a place where you love to live."

- Roofer: "A roof done right is watertight, but a roof done wrong won't last too long!"

- Therapist: "I have the owner's manual for your mind."

- Water filter representative: "Either buy a filter or be a filter."

I've always believed that Memory Hooks like these were money in the bank. One day, before starting a workshop I was giving in Glendale, California, for about sixty business people, I watched as a young dentist stood and gave his brief introduction to the assembled group: "I'm a dentist. I believe in the tooth, the whole tooth, and nothing but the tooth, so help me God." After everyone finished laughing, he gave his name and phone number and sat down. I thought this was the perfect opportunity to test my theory regarding people remembering Memory Hook presentations better than other presentations. So later in the morning, when I was talking to the group about the importance of well-thought-out presentations, I asked for them to all stand. When they were all standing, I asked them, on the count of three, to point to the person who believed in "the tooth, the whole tooth, and nothing but the tooth, so help me God." Not much to my surprise, all sixty people pointed to the dentist, without hesitation!

♦ *If you take the time to develop good presentations, people will take notice. If you don't, you are losing a great opportunity to someone else who will.*

If you take the time to develop good presentations, people will take notice. If you don't, you are losing a great opportunity to someone else who will.

## DON'T FENCE YOURSELF IN

While it's important to be specific about the products or services you offer, take care not to limit your potential market by what you say. I encountered a man who said that he offered an "incentive program for companies wanting to reward employees for their performance." I knew, however, that he offered a catalog of products to companies interested in giving the products as incentives. Had he described his fabulous catalog and the wondrous results that companies achieved by offering the gifts within it as incentives, he would have had better results.

## LOWEST COMMON DENOMINATOR

**B**y breaking your product or service down to its most basic form, or Lowest Common Denominator (LCD), you will be able to effectively describe to other people the type of work you do. What is most basic about what you do?

◆ A specific product or service?

◆ A selected target market?

◆ Unique benefits to a particular group?

◆ Your qualifications as a professional in your industry?

Handouts, or if applicable, samples that you can show and discuss, help you make a strong impression. The more things people can see, hear, feel, and touch, the more likely they are to remember your message. The more they remember, the more likely they are to refer you. The Hand-to-Hand WOMBAT Plan in the back of this book has a worksheet to help you prepare your Memory Hooks and LCDs. If you don't have support materials to accompany these, start creating them.

> ◆ *The more things people can see, hear, feel, and touch, the more likely they are to remember your message.*

As you make presentations, always consider the needs of your audience and limit your discussion primarily to those areas. If you're giving a short presentation to a large group, focus on the part of your business you think will benefit most of the group. If you're talking to only one or two people, find out as much as you can about them.

## MAKE NO ASSUMPTIONS

**M**any people make the fatal mistake of assuming that others know a lot about their business. I heard a florist tell a networking group, "I'm not sure what else to say. You all know what a florist does, right?" Wrong! We didn't know the variety of services and products this florist provided. He knew his business and assumed that everyone else knew it as well. Later, I asked him whether his shop was an FTD florist, and

- Did he accept credit cards?
- Did he offer seasonal specials for holidays? If so, which ones?
- Did he handle emergency orders?
- Could he do a good job for weddings?
- Did he give a discount to members?
- Could I set up a billing arrangement with his company?
- Did he have an 800 number?
- Could I order by fax?
- Do certain colors of roses signify certain things?
- What type of arrangement was appropriate for a graduation?
- Could he give me any tips on keeping flowers alive longer?
- What was his most challenging order?

I told him there were hundreds of things I didn't know about his business, and others surely felt the same way. Not using his time before the group to tell everyone something about his service was an opportunity lost.

Everyone has something he can say that will educate people about the services he has to offer. Don't pass up a chance to teach people more about what you do.

+ *Don't pass up opportunities to teach people more about what you do.*

## PRESENTATION PREPARATION

**W**rite out your presentation and refine what you've written, several times if necessary. Preparing an effective, brief introduction with a strong Memory Hook can usually be done without a lot of effort.

Next, practice your presentation on someone you know before using it at your next networking group. When your test audience understands what you have to offer and likes the way you present it, you're ready for larger arenas.

It is impossible to have a Positive Message, Delivered Effectively if you don't prepare presentations and practice them in the networking environments you participate in.

## HOT TIPS AND INSIGHTS

**1** The ideal introduction is brief and memorable, one that provides enough impact to arouse the interest of those you're introducing yourself to.

**2** What you do and say sets the pattern for duplication. Like the telephone game, you need to constantly check down the line to ensure that your original message is being passed along accurately.

**3** If you want to be a Notable Networker, you have to get the most out of your first sixty seconds. Take the time to plan your introduction and prepare some concise and descriptive overviews of your product or service.

**4** The recommended sequence for your scripts is your name, your business or profession, a brief description of your business or profession, a Memory Hook, and a benefit statement.

**5** Develop several scripts that you can readily use when attending networking meetings.

6. Use Memory Hooks to increase the probability that people will recall what you do. A good Memory Hook doesn't need to be funny, but it helps.

7. The more things people can see, hear, feel, and touch, the more likely they'll remember your message. The more they remember, the more likely they are to refer you.

8. Take the time to break down your product or service to its Lowest Common Denominators: specific products, target markets, unique benefits, etc.

9. Everyone has something he or she can say that will educate people about the services he or she has to offer. Never pass up an opportunity to teach people more about what you do.

10. Practice your presentation on someone you know before using it at your next networking group.

### Chapter 12

# Mastering the Mixer

## *The Ten Commandments*

### GETTING THE MOST FROM CASUAL CONTACTS

**M**aking contacts that turn into relationships is the foundation of a prosperous word-of-mouth business. Neophyte networkers repeatedly ask me, "What can I do to meet more people and make better contacts at business mixers?" To answer this important question, I've put together what I call the "Ten Commandments of Networking

## THE TEN COMMANDMENTS
## OF NETWORKING A MIXER

1. Have your networking tools with you at all times.
2. Set a goal for the number of people you'll meet.
3. Act like a host, not a guest.
4. Listen, and ask the five "W" questions: who, what, where, when, and why.
5. Give a lead or referral whenever possible.
6. Describe your product or service in sixty seconds.
7. Exchange business cards with the people you meet.
8. Spend ten minutes or less with each person you meet.
9. Write comments on the backs of the business cards you collect.
10. Follow up with the people you meet.

a Mixer." These rules work just as well for events like a Chamber of Commerce mixer as a company open-house party.

By their nature, mixers present Casual Contact opportunities, so you need to use different techniques than for Strong Contact Networks, service clubs, or professional associations.

## COMMANDMENT 1: HAVE YOUR NETWORKING
## TOOLS WITH YOU AT ALL TIMES

The first of the ten commandments is to have with you at all times the tools you need to network. This is the foundation of all that follows. All successful business people have the "tools of the trade." Notable Networkers' tools include an informative name badge, plenty of business cards, brochures about their business, and a pocket-sized business-card file that has the business cards of the professionals they refer.

As an effective networker, you need to purchase a commercially made badge. These look more professional than the stick-on, "Hello My Name Is" paper badges. Your badge needs to include both your name and your company's name or your profession on it. As a rule of thumb, use your company's name if it describes your profession. For example:

# John Anderson

### *"READY-FAST"*
### *PRINT & COPY*

If your company's name does not clearly describe your profession (as is the case with a consulting firm like Carlton, Donner, & Finch), write your profession on the badge:

## *Mary S. Carlton*

### ADVERTISING &
### MARKETING CONSULTANT

Badges are now available that require only slipping your business card into the top and — voilà! — instant badge! These badges are unique because you are literally wearing your business card, logo and all.

Make sure the print on your card is readable to people standing a few feet away. Many people recommend wearing your badge on the right side, because people shake right-handed and the badge is easier to see. While this seems to makes sense, if you're that close to someone, it doesn't matter much. Always look for a profession on the badge. Knowing someone's profession or company name makes it easier to start a dialogue, because you can ask about his or her business. Always carry plenty of business cards with you. I like to stash some in my wallet, briefcase, calendar, and car so that I'm never without them. I also keep a small metal card holder in the coat pocket of each of my suits.

## COMMANDMENT 2: SET A GOAL FOR THE NUMBER OF PEOPLE YOU'LL MEET

Some people go to a meeting with only one goal in mind: the time they plan to leave! To get the most out of a networking event, set a goal regarding the number of contacts you want to make or the number of business cards you want to collect. Don't leave until you've met your goal.

If you feel inspired, set a goal to meet fifteen to twenty people and make sure you get all their cards. If you don't feel so hot, shoot for less. In either case, set a reachable goal based on the attendance and type of group.

## COMMANDMENT 3: ACT LIKE A HOST, NOT A GUEST

In her book *Skills for Success*, Dr. Adele Scheele tells about a cocktail party where she met someone who was hesitant to introduce himself to total strangers. Dr. Scheele suggested that he "consider a different scenario for the evening. That is, consider himself the party's host instead of its guest." She asked him, if he were the host, wouldn't he introduce himself to people he didn't know and then introduce them to each other? Wouldn't he make sure people knew where the food and drinks were? Wouldn't he watch for lulls in conversations, or bring new people over to an already-formed small group?

Scheele's new acquaintance acknowledged the obvious difference between the active role of the host and the passive role of the guest. A host is expected to do things for others, while a guest sits back and relaxes. Scheele concluded that "there was nothing to stop this man from playing the role of host even though he wasn't the actual host." There is nothing to stop you from being far more active when you're with a large group of people, either.

Along this line, I recommend that you volunteer to be an Ambassador, or Visitor Host, at the networking groups you belong to. An Ambassador or Visitor Host is someone who greets all the visitors and introduces them to others. If you see visitors sitting, introduce yourself and ask if they would like to meet other members.

If there are many other visitors to meet, ask another member to help you by introducing the visitor to the rest of the membership so that *you* can get back to meeting new visitors. By using this technique, you'll start to develop excellent networking skills and get great exposure to many business professionals in a short time.

A distinguishing characteristic of self-made millionaires, according to Thomas Stanley, professor of marketing at Georgia State University, is that they network everywhere. Most important, they do it all the time — at business conferences, at the health club, on the golf course, or with the person sitting next to them on a plane. This fact alone should motivate you to place yourself in situations where you can meet new people.

Sit between strangers at business meetings or strike up a conversation with people at the spa. Make friends, even when you don't need to.

## COMMANDMENT 4: LISTEN, AND ASK THE FIVE "W" QUESTIONS: WHO, WHAT, WHERE, WHEN, AND WHY

**A**s Dale Carnegie advised, show genuine interest in the other person's business. If I meet a printer, I ask, "What kind of printing do you specialize in? Commercial? Four-color? Instant? Copying? Where are you located? How long have you been in business?"

The answer to each of these questions gives me a better grasp of the individual and the type of work she does. Thus, I'm in a better position to refer her to others or invite her to different networking groups.

## COMMANDMENT 5: GIVE A REFERRAL WHENEVER POSSIBLE

**N**otable Networkers believe in the "givers gain" philosophy. If you don't genuinely attempt to help the people you meet, then you are not networking. You need to be creative in this area.

Few of the people you meet for the first time at a business mixer are going to express a need for your product or service. That doesn't mean you can't give them something.

If you can't give people bona fide referrals, offer them some information that would be of interest to them. Tell them about a speaker's bureau in their area that could help them get speaking engagements, tell them about another business mixer that's coming up soon, or give them information about one of the networking organizations you belong to. Don't be a "narcoleptic networker." Stay awake, and take an active role in the networking groups you belong to.

If you work hard at developing your skills, people will remember you in a positive way. In addition, you will ultimately expand your Contact Sphere, because, as we discussed earlier, many people who start out as Casual Contacts become Strong Contacts.

The larger your network, the better your chances of reaching out and calling upon resources you wouldn't have access to otherwise. Most important, with this growth comes increased visibility, exposure, opportunity, and success.

## COMMANDMENT 6: DESCRIBE YOUR PRODUCT OR SERVICE

A fter you've learned what other people do, make sure to tell them what you do. Be specific but brief; use Memory Hooks or LCDs. Whatever you do, don't assume they know your business. Explain it to them if they seem interested.

## COMMANDMENT 7: EXCHANGE BUSINESS CARDS WITH THE PEOPLE YOU MEET

A sk the person you've just met for two of his cards, one to pass on to someone else and one to keep for yourself. This sets the stage for networking to happen. Keep your cards in one pocket and put other people's cards in the other pocket. This way, you won't be fumbling around trying to find your cards while accidentally giving somebody else's card away. What do you do with business cards you collect from people you meet at networking events such as business forums, breakfasts, and mixers? These cards can be instrumental in helping you remember people, initiate follow-ups, discover opportunities, and access information and resources.

Always review the cards for pertinent information. It is not always easy to determine what people do simply from their title or company name. Note whether the products and services offered by the company are listed or summarized. If you've just received the card of an attorney, check to see whether the card indicates the attorney's specialty. To demonstrate your interest, write the missing information you collect on the front of the card, in view of the other person.

## COMMANDMENT 8: SPEND TEN MINUTES OR LESS WITH EACH PERSON YOU MEET AND DON'T LINGER WITH FRIENDS AND ASSOCIATES

**R**ecalling Commandment 2, if your goal is to meet a given number of people, then you can't spend too much time with any one person, no matter how interesting the conversation gets. Stay focused on making as many contacts as you can. When you meet people who are very interesting and with whom you want to spend more time, set up appointments with them. You can always meet later to continue the conversation.

Don't try to close business deals while you're networking; it's impractical. Set a date to meet and discuss your product or service in an environment more conducive to doing business. You may be able to increase your business with hot prospects if you take the time to fully understand their needs.

Learn to leave conversations gracefully. Honesty is usually the best policy; tell them you need to connect with a few more people, sample the hors d'oeuvres, or get another drink. If you feel uncomfortable with that, exit like a host by introducing new acquaintances to someone you know. Better yet, if it seems appropriate, ask them to introduce you to people they know.

Above all, don't linger with friends and associates! These are people you already know, and you're there to meet people you don't know. I attended a mixer once where I saw several business friends stand and talk with one another for two hours. On their way out, one actually complained, "This was a waste of time. I didn't get any business from it, did you?" No kidding.

## COMMANDMENT 9: WRITE COMMENTS ON THE BACKS OF THE BUSINESS CARDS YOU COLLECT

**T**his helps you remember more about the person when you follow up the next day. I try to meet many people when I'm at a mixer. Two hours and twenty people later, I can't always keep everyone straight. Therefore, I always carry a pen, and when I've concluded a conversation with a new acquaintance, I step away and jot down notes, including the date and location of the event. This information is crucial for effective follow-up and becomes more important the busier you are. I also write a note about what the person is seeking; for example:

"... wants to visit BNI,"

"... looking for a good printer,"

"... has friend moving out of the area and needs a real-estate agent," or the most important one of all,

"... wants to set an appointment with me; call on Tuesday."

If the individual doesn't express a specific need, I may write down something about him or her that I learned from the conversation — things relating to his or her responsibilities, contacts, interests, or hobbies. For example:

"... likes to back-pack,"

"... knows Joe Smith from L.A.," or

"... supervises ten employees."

Record *anything* you think may be useful in remembering the person more clearly. As you'll see in Commandment 10, the more information you have about the people you meet, the better your chances of a successful follow-up.

## COMMANDMENT 10: FOLLOW UP WITH THE PEOPLE YOU MEET

I've seen people spend untold hours in networking organizations, yet fail at networking because their follow-up was appalling. Remember, good follow-up is the lifeblood of networking. You can obey the previous nine commandments religiously, but if you don't follow up effectively, you're wasting your time!

If you promise to get back to people, make sure you do. Even if you don't promise, call them or drop them a letter. If you follow up effectively, networking can be empowering.

Copy the list of commandments at the start of this chapter and keep it with you in your calendar, briefcase, or purse. The next time you go to a business mixer, review the list before you go inside.

This chapter is part of the core of creating a positive message and delivering it effectively. Establishing a word-of-mouth-based business requires getting out of your cave and getting belly to belly with other business professionals. The next time you have the opportunity to go to a gathering of this sort, keep the Ten Commandments of Networking a Mixer in mind.

## HOT TIPS AND INSIGHTS

**1** Purchase a commercially made badge, and always bring plenty of business cards.

**2** To get the most out of a networking event, set yourself a goal for the number of contacts you will make, or the number of business cards you want to collect. Don't leave until you've met your goal.

**3** Act like a host, not a guest. There's nothing to stop you from being far more active when you're with a large group of people. Volunteer to be a Visitor Host at the networking groups you belong to.

**4** Keep asking questions about what the other person does.

**5** If you can't give people a bona fide referral, offer other information that would be of interest to them.

**6** After you've learned what the other person does, make sure to tell her what you do. Be specific but brief.

**7** Exchange business cards with the people you meet.

**8** Stay focused on making as many contacts as you can; don't linger with friends and associates! Don't try to close business deals while you're networking; it's impractical.

**9** Write comments on the business cards you collect. Good follow-up is the lifeblood of networking. If you promise to get back to someone, make sure you do it.

### Chapter 13

# Hosting a Business Mixer

*Nuts and Bolts for a Successful Event*

## ANATOMY OF A SUCCESSFUL BUSINESS MIXER

**I**f you have a large enough office, throwing a business mixer at your office is a great way to get exposure for your business. It's a bold step, but I recommend that you go to one of your networking groups and offer to hold a mixer at your company. Because many business groups, such as Chambers of Commerce, sometimes charge participants a small fee to pay for the food, it might not even cost you anything to host the event. Even if it does, spending a little money to get dozens of people into your office is generally worth the expense.

Let's look at the important elements of throwing a successful business mixer.

Plan the mixer no less than eight weeks in advance. Since your purpose is to meet new people, concentrate on inviting as many guests as you can. Talk up the event and make sure your network group is actively supporting it. Have your group set aside the date on their calendars so they can begin to invite guests. Get people (including yourself) to donate door prizes for the mixer.

> ◆ *Even if it costs money, getting dozens of people to come to your office is generally worth the expense.*

You need to have a good idea of what the attendance will be and get early commitments. Print invitations well in advance and require RSVPs. Tell guests there will be a brochure table at the mixer, and suggest they bring information on their products or services. Have one or more large tables set aside with a sign for this purpose.

Designate several Visitor Hosts to greet the guests as they arrive. When people start to arrive, make sure they fill out their name tags properly (name as well as business or profession). Have few chairs available, so people will circulate rather than sit.

Conduct a short networking exercise or two, such as having each guest meet three people he hasn't met before or find someone in a similar business and ask what networking techniques work best for him or her. The key is to get everyone to mingle and meet people; networking exercises give everyone license to do precisely that. For those people you don't think will participate, jokingly tell everyone that some guy named "Bruno" will be at the door to ensure that everyone has collected other people's cards before leaving the building! If you have to announce anything at the mixer, keep it short — it's a mixer, not a meeting.

## IDEAS FOR A VIBRANT MIXER

**T**here are many innovative things you can do to make a mixer both fun and successful. One idea is to conduct a "Meet Your (Business) Match" mixer wherein you set up designated areas for specific business professions, such as health care, real estate, finance, business consulting, advertising/marketing, art, fashion, computer products, and so on. Mark these sections clearly and post someone in each area to get things rolling. The areas would be visited by people interested in

- learning more about those topics,
- needing those services, or
- wanting to talk to others in the same field.

Another idea is to have everyone pick a card with a name of one person from a famous duo out of a hat. For example, if I picked "Hammerstein," then my goal would be to keep meeting people until I ran into the person who picked "Rodgers." Others combos include

- Punch and Judy
- Minnie and Mickey
- Marx and Lenin
- Lennon and McCartney
- Boris and Natasha
- Bill and Hillary
- Lewis and Clark
- Frankie and Annette
- Napoleon and Josephine
- Salt and Pepper
- Tom and Jerry
- Bonnie and Clyde
- Romeo and Juliet
- Caesar and Cleopatra
- Gilbert and Sullivan

## NETWORKING AEROBICS

Networking is like exercising; if you don't keep at it, you lose what you've started to develop. Here are some tongue-in-cheek exercises that will tone up your networking abilities:

*Dead-weight lifts:* This is where you "lift" some dead weight (your body) out of bed, or off the couch, and go to the network meetings you need to be attending.

*High hurdles:* Overcoming the introduction jitters when you first start meeting people at a mixer. Almost everyone has to deal with the high hurdles at some time. The best approach to this is to "jump in."

*Floor exercise:* Working your way in and out of crowds with grace and precision, showing everyone how Notable Networking is done.

*Relays:* This is the part of the meeting where you use your business card as a baton to be passed from person to person.

*Leg lifts:* Involves lifting your legs and walking around a networking event, not allowing yourself to stand idle for more than a couple of minutes.

*Buttocks lift:* This is a critical networking aerobics exercise involving lifting your tush off the seat and mingling.

*The splits:* This exercise dictates that if you are at a networking meeting that requires you to sit down for some part of the meeting, then you cannot sit between two people you already know.

*Arm extension:* An exercise in which you extend your arm, "press some flesh" (shake hands), and meet people.

*Jaw flex:* This immediately follows the arm extension — telling people who you are and what you do.

*Lift and carry:* After you've talked with each person, collect his or her card and carry this large stack home with you.

*Arm curls:* This is the most important exercise of all. A few days after the mixer, pick up a phone in either hand, turn the receiver to face you, curl it up to your ear, and call the people you recently met.

Figure 13.1. Networking Aerobics Instructions

This exercise gets people mixing in a hurry. If you'd like another idea on getting people to mingle, hand out the Networking Aerobics instructions shown in figure 13.1.

I wrote these exercises for fun; however, don't mistake the importance of the issues I'm addressing. You can't network effectively from your couch. You may not feel like going to network meetings sometimes, but attending these events reminds people who you are and what you do. If you stop going to the meetings, eventually people will forget about you and turn to others, often to people they've met recently at meetings you should have attended.

## BUSINESS CARD BINGO

Another effective people-mixing technique, "Business Card Bingo," gets participants to make many solid contacts in one night (fig. 13.2). First, you drop your business card in the "bingo box," as does everyone else. You are then placed at a table with other people with whom you've asked to sit, or who were assigned at random. Each person receives a "bingo card" and writes his name in the center square.

Next, everyone follows a set of structured networking exercises and circulates throughout the room. To complete the bingo card, each participant meets twenty-four other people, collects their business cards, and has them write their names in the open squares. Then the names on the business cards that everyone dropped in the bingo box are called (or better yet, listed on a big flip chart or sign so that everyone can keep networking). Regular bingo rules apply thereafter.

The winner is the first person with five names in a row, either across, down, or diagonally. Of course, everybody wins, because everyone makes new contacts.

# BUSINESS CARD
# B I N G O

|  |  |  |  |  |
|---|---|---|---|---|
|  |  |  |  |  |
|  |  |  |  |  |
|  |  | Your Name |  |  |
|  |  |  |  |  |
|  |  |  |  |  |

## RULES OF THE GAME

1. Drop your business card into the "bingo box."
2. Sign your own name legibly in the middle square.
3. Circulate and introduce yourself to other guests.
4. Get other guests to fill your remaining squares with their legible signatures.
5. Business cards (instead of numbers) will be drawn.
6. Regular bingo rules apply (across/down/diagonal).

**Figure 13.2.** Business Card Bingo                    © 1989 Ivan R. Misner

## STAY FOCUSED ON MIXING

T hrowing a successful business mixer isn't easy. However, if you remember that your primary purpose is to facilitate networking, you'll be okay. There is a Chamber of Commerce in the San Gabriel Valley (which shall remain anonymous) that I refuse to visit anymore because their mixers are a farce. It's not because of their attendance; they actually draw a pretty good-sized crowd. It's because their director can't get off the microphone, making it difficult for anyone to network.

About an hour or so into the mixer, he usually starts yelling, "QUIET! QUIET! QUIET! . . . I NEED EVERYONE'S ATTENTION!" Then he starts introducing people for one reason after another, usually in bunches of ten at a time, for thirty minutes or more (one night I expected him to introduce his wife and kids). The sin in all this is that people are no longer allowed to "mix" at the mixer.

After a few minutes, everyone begins ignoring the speaker and trying to continue conversations in a low whisper. Then the whisper gradually becomes a roar and, you guessed it, the director again yells, "QUIET! QUIET! QUIET, PLEASE!" Here's the bottom line on presentations at mixers: if you're going to give speeches, hold a meeting; if you're going to have a mixer, don't give speeches.

At the end of the mixer, spend no more than about ten minutes or so doing introductions and giving the door prizes.

This chapter is another part of the core process of creating a positive message and delivering it effectively. Establishing a word-of-mouth-based business sometimes requires getting people to come to your cave to learn more about your products and services.

## HOT TIPS AND INSIGHTS

**1** If you have a large enough office, throw a business mixer there to get exposure for your business.

**2** Plan the mixer no less than eight weeks in advance. Invite many guests and get people to donate door prizes.

**3** Allow all to bring information on their products or services. Have one or more large tables set aside with a sign for this purpose.

**4** Designate several "Visitor Hosts" to greet the guests as they arrive. When people start to arrive, make sure all fill out their name tags properly. Have *few* chairs available.

**5** Conduct a short networking exercise, such as having each guest meet three people he hasn't met before or having everyone find someone in a similar business and ask what has worked for him in networking.

**6** There are many innovative things you can do to make a mixer both fun and successful, such as have a "Meet Your (Business) Match" mixer, with designated areas for specific business professions, such as finance, real estate, health care, etc. Or have everyone pick a card with the name of one half of a famous duo out of a hat. Then each person keeps meeting people until he or she runs into his or her "partner."

**7** Throwing a successful business mixer isn't easy. However, if you remember that your primary purpose is to facilitate networking, you'll be okay.

**8** At the end of the mixer, spend no more than about ten minutes doing introductions and giving door prizes.

### Chapter 14

# The Referral Boomerang

*What Goes Around,*
*Comes Around*

## GATEKEEPERS

**T**here are people of a specific type, found in most communities, that you should emulate. I call them "gatekeepers." Gatekeepers are movers and shakers in the community. Most of us know at least one gatekeeper; indeed, gatekeepers are the type who seem to know everyone. More important, they are adept at getting people together.

In effect, they stand by a gate of contacts and referrals and open it, as needed, to put people with common needs and interests together.

Gatekeepers are almost always successful in their fields. The reason should be obvious. They are willing to help people who need referrals, ideas, contacts, or assistance. By giving help to so many others, they find that it comes back to them in return. Your goal should be to become a gatekeeper: someone others go to when they are looking for the right connection.

*♦ Strive to become a gatekeeper — someone others go to when they are looking for the right connection.*

There's no quick formula for becoming a gatekeeper; it may take years. Rest assured that following through on the suggestions in this book will greatly accelerate your progress. Being a gatekeeper is a state of mind and a philosophy of doing business that will come back to you in many positive ways.

Edie Fraser, president of the Public Affairs Group, is one of the best-known gatekeepers in Washington, D.C. Edie is practically a one-woman information clearing house. She is always matching people with complementary interests, and her firm gets dozens of calls every day from people who know that she'll have the right answer or contact for them. Does it lead to more business for Edie's firm? Yes. She's increased her staff size five years in a row and recently relocated to larger offices.

Over the last decade, I've met many business professionals who have built their business not on the failure of others but on the success of others. They have done it by creating a reputation for not only knowing people but being able to get them together. Most important, they are very active at passing bona fide referrals to the people they've developed relationships with. The foundation of building a word-of-mouth-based business involves giving referrals to others as well as connecting people so that they may increase their business.

## THE BOOMERANG EFFECT

**B**uilding a word-of-mouth-based business means, among other things, knowing how to give good referrals. If you give referrals consistently to others, you will be one of those individuals who enjoy the Boomerang Effect — having a referral you threw out to someone else come back in the form of new business for you. Having been on the receiving end of the Boomerang Effect many times, I can honestly tell you it feels great! For example, several years ago I received a referral from someone in Los Angeles to whom I had sent business in the past. The referral not only did business with me but referred at least three other people from all over the U.S. who have also done business with me. This particular boomerang keeps coming back, again and again.

◆ *Sometimes a referral you gave someone else boomerangs as new business for you.*

Actively listen for people to express a need represented by someone in your personal network of contacts. A good networker has two ears and one mouth and uses them proportionately. Listen to what people have to say, then refer someone to them whenever they have a need that you can help with.

Remember that a referral is not a guaranteed sale but an opportunity to discuss business with someone in the market to buy or use a particular product or service. You should view referrals as either hot, warm, or tepid:

- ◆ A "hot referral" is someone actively looking for a product or service now, and willing to have the person you know call to discuss it.

- ◆ A "warm referral" is someone who has been shopping around, but is willing to talk to another provider of that product or service.

- ◆ A "tepid referral" is someone who expresses an interest or wants to talk to the person you know, but isn't in the market to proceed right now.

## FIVE POINTERS ON GIVING REFERRALS

**S**ince business referrals are the principal tools and the valued currency of networking, you should make sure that yours are both timely and appropriate. Here are five important points to consider in giving a good referral:

1.   Listen for needs from the people you meet. When you meet someone who expresses a need, tell her you know a person of business that can provide that product or service. Tell her about your business experience, if any, with that person. Give her the business card of the person you're referring, and ask for hers.

2.   Ask whether it is okay for the person or business you are referring to call. This helps determine how hot the referral is. If she says yes, fill out a referral slip (or use the back of your card) and give it to the person you referred.

3.   When giving a referral to someone, be careful not to misrepresent the quality of the referral. Your honesty about the prospect will be appreciated, even if the referral is tepid.

4.   Whenever you have a hot referral for someone, don't hang onto it. Call the person you've referred right away; hot referrals have a way of cooling off quickly. Provide as much information as possible about the prospect, including the prospect's name, address, phone number, occupation, and any relevant information about the product or service the prospect is looking for.

5.   Avoid giving bad referrals, such as

- ◆   News about a meeting for business owners, a chamber mixer, or any other business meeting. This is an announcement, and potentially good information to have, but *not* a referral.

- ◆   Providing someone with a better source for obtaining products. Again, this is good information for someone, but not a business referral.

- Giving the same referral to three different people in the same profession.

- Referring someone to a prospect without telling the prospect that you have done so.

- Giving someone a referral but telling him or her not to use your name with the prospect.

## STAY ON TOP OF YOUR CONTACTS

Connect with people outside of business meetings whenever you can. Write cards or letters, send articles that might be of interest, call to check in, or invite them to a local business meeting you're going to attend.

Monitor the referrals you give. This tells you how often you're giving referrals, and to whom. Having this information helps you focus on helping some individual who has helped you a great deal in the past.

Becoming proficient at giving referrals should be one of your main goals. Each time you're going to buy a product or service, think first about the people in your network; this is what you would want them to do for you. In order to remember the wide variety of services offered by the members of your own personal network, maintain a large file containing copies of the literature they hand out. Even more important, keep a large card file with several copies of all your strong networking contacts. This will enable you to actually hand out their cards whenever you refer them to a prospect who needs their services. Helping others deliver their message effectively inevitably helps you, because there is no truer statement relating to word of mouth than "What goes around, comes around."

## HOT TIPS AND INSIGHTS

**1** A gatekeeper is a mover and shaker in the community, adept at getting people together. Your goal is to become a gatekeeper, someone others go to when they are looking for the right connection.

**2** Remember the Boomerang Effect: having a referral you threw out to someone else come back in the form of new business for you.

**3** A good networker has two ears and one mouth and uses them proportionately.

**4** Connect with people outside of business meetings whenever you can. Write cards or letters, send articles that might be of interest, call to check in, and invite them to accompany you to a local business meeting.

**5** In giving a good referral, listen for needs from the people you meet; ask whether it's okay to have the person you're referring call; make sure others have realistic expectations about the quality of the referrals you provide; don't hang onto a hot referral for someone; and avoid giving bad referrals.

**6** Monitor the referrals you give. This tells you how often you're giving referrals, and to whom. Having this information helps you focus on helping people who have helped you in the past.

### Chapter 15

# **A**ttracting Hot Referrals

## *The Keys to Getting Good Word of Mouth*

### BEGIN BY ASKING FOR THEM

I t always amazes me, when I speak with business professionals looking for referrals, to find out that they haven't really asked their friends, associates, networking partners, customers, clients, or patients for a referral. Mind you, most people will initially say they've asked for referrals, but when I've probed, I found that they asked for referrals from a very small percentage of their contacts. Having not received a favorable response, they've pretty much dropped the effort.

A very effective approach for asking someone for a referral is outlined in a book called *Referrals,* by Mark Sheer. In his book, Mark strongly recommends that the phrase you need to use when asking for a referral is "I'm expanding my business and I need your help. Who do you know who . . . ?" Mark goes on to say:

> *You must NOT alter this phrase.* It has been tried and proven successful. Other phrases have been tried and have not produced the desired results — so don't waste your time using them. Once you become comfortable with this new phrase, it is very easy to ask your contact for a referral by simply saying, "Who do you know who . . . ?"

This approach provides you with an open-ended question format that allows people to think about the ways they may be able to refer to you. Most people who do not get a positive response to their request for referrals fail because they have asked a very specific closed-ended question such as, "Do you know anyone who needs my service?"

Ironically, while I was writing the material for this chapter I received a letter from a woman from whom I had purchased some children's educational toys over the years. She had obviously taken one of Mark's seminars, because I received the following letter (italics mine):

> Dear Dr. Misner:

> Just a note to thank you for your business and support. I am expanding my business and I need your help. *Who do you know who* matches my ideal customer profile? I would be thrilled if you would take a few minutes to make a list of acquaintances and friends who could benefit from my services; people and companies you believe want or need the quality service and follow-up I will provide. Please read and fill out the enclosed "Customer Profile." I will give you a call by the end of the week. In the meantime, please feel free to send in the profile using the enclosed self-addressed stamped envelope. Thank you in advance.

*Who do you know who* is having a baby?

*Who do you know who* is a new parent, grandparent, aunt or uncle?

*Who do you know who* needs developmental toys for their children?

*Who do you know who* belongs to an organization or group that donates to children's groups, such as Toys for Tots, Pediatric AIDS Foundation, etc.?

*Who do you know who* is a teacher?

*Who do you know who* wants a career that directly affects the future of the world through the education of children?

> Sincerely,
>
> S.L.
> Educational Toys Consultant

By listing people who I know fit the description she outlined above, I'm giving her tacit approval to use my name when she contacts them. The only thing better than this would be for me to say something to them myself.

## THE VALUE OF TESTIMONIALS

An important part of having a Positive Message, Delivered Effectively is knowing how to cultivate relationships in such a way as to have others talking about you positively. Having someone tell a group of people how good your product or service is beats anything you can say about yourself. This is called a "testimonial." Many years ago, a chiropractor who was a member of BNI asked me what he could do to start getting some business from his chapter. I asked him if anyone in the chapter had ever used his services. He said no. I asked him if anyone in the group had ever used any chiropractor. He said probably not.

I told him that the best way for him to get some business was to get at least one member to use his services. Chiropractic care, like any form of health care, is personal. I suggested that he offer a special members-only discount that would persuade at least one member to use his services.

At the next meeting, he announced that he would take insurance as payment in full. Thus, anyone covered by a major medical plan would pay nothing to use him. Only one person took him up on this generous offer; the chiropractor was disappointed.

At the following meeting, the member who had recently used his services stood up and addressed the group. "I went to our chiropractor this week and all I can say is that I have been an IDIOT! I can't believe that I've waited all these years to go see a chiropractor. This guy is GREAT! You're all CRAZY if you don't take him up on his offer. I've always had this little back problem. I didn't think it was any big deal, but I didn't know how much this thing was bothering me until it wasn't there any more. I FEEL GREAT!"

When he sat down, another member joked, "What the heck, he's still walking, I guess I'll try it too." The following week, this member came to the meeting and gave the chiropractor a good referral for another client. In short, the chiropractor received four new clients in a couple of weeks, all because someone stood up and said, "I've used his services and you should too, *because....*"

♦ *Ask people who have used your products or services to talk to others about their experience.*

I've highlighted the word "because" so that you will understand that an effective testimonial is good only if someone is *specific* about the person's service or product and provides details as to why it was good and how it helped. Such testimonials become shared experiences with the others present, thus putting everyone much more at ease about the service or product being offered.

Ask people who have used your products or services to talk to others about their experience. In addition, whenever possible, have them give you a testimonial letter you can use when speaking to people they know.

It's important as well for you to give testimonials about the people and the businesses you've used. In their book *Putting the One-Minute Manager to Work,* Ken Blanchard and Robert Lorber say that feedback on perfor-
mance is one of the most crucial elements in dealing effectively with people. They suggest that feedback reinforces continued good performance. When you have a chance to give a testimo-nial, you should talk about the services or products you've used; be specific about how it worked out. In a meeting environ-ment, simply giving everyone a laundry list of the people you've used doesn't help anyone.

◆ *When you have a chance to give a testimonial, be specific about how the products or services worked out.*

If you're active in various business networking groups, especially Strong Contact Networks, you'll find that testimoni-als are an integral element of the process. It's important not only to receive them but to give them as well. Testimonials add credibility and trust to those with whom you are trying to build a word-of-mouth-based business. In addition to testimonials, however, there are other things you should consider in making sure you get your fair share of referrals.

## SUPPORT MATERIAL AND TECHNIQUES

**B**elow are some effective ways to influence people to refer you. Some of these may not work for everyone. The idea is to select those you think you can apply in your own business or profession.

**Samples.** If you have an opportunity to distribute your materials, do it. Bring products, samples, brochures, or a presen-tation book. Many networking groups provide a brochure table where you can place these items. If people can see, feel, touch, hear, or smell samples of the product or service you provide, they are more likely to use you. Offer special, members-only prices or services. If you can get network members to use you, then, like the chiropractor, they are much more likely to refer you.

**Presentation books.** Everyone active in networking groups can benefit by developing a presentation book. Buy a high-quality, three-ring binder that can attractively display samples of your products or services, brochures, photographs, etc. Take this to your meetings and make sure it gets circulated.

**Free presentations or demonstrations.** Many business professionals offer to speak free of charge to service clubs or business organizations as a way of getting exposure and promoting their business. If your product or service is conducive to this approach, tell the members of your personal network that you offer this service, and accept speaking engagements as bona fide referrals. Ask them to pitch you to the program chairs of organizations to which they belong.

If you're well prepared and do a good job at these presentations, you may find yourself getting many more speaking offers and a lot of new business. This technique is effective for almost any profession, but is particularly helpful for consultants, therapists, financial planners, CPAs, and attorneys.

**Door prizes.** Smart business professionals know that people who have tried their products or services will probably use them again. I highly recommend that you offer door prizes regularly at your networking groups and ensure that you are given credit for the door prize when it is given. Always attach a business card so the winner knows where to get more.

**Keep in touch regularly.** Meet people outside of the normal meetings that you go to whenever you can. Write cards or letters, send articles that might be of interest, call to check in, let them know about a local business mixer, have lunch, play racquetball, tennis, or golf. Reinforce the relationship with thank-yous. If someone gives you a referral or important information, send a thank-you note or gift basket. This reinforcement will strengthen the bond and encourage that person to think of you again.

## Follow-Up

K nowing how to get referrals is really a matter of knowing how to be helpful to the people you associate with and how to ask for help in return. A successful word-of-mouth program involves creating an effective support system for yourself that also works to the advantage of others.

All the networking in the world, however, serves no purpose if you don't follow up effectively with the people you meet or who are referred to you. I've seen people who work hard at making contacts but whose follow-up was so bad that the contacts were lost. It's as if they networked halfway and completely lost sight of the potential to generate word-of-mouth business. Follow-up letters and phone calls set the stage for further contact. All things being equal, the more you're in contact with others, the more business you'll generate. Today, more than ever, there's no excuse for not following up. Why? Because there are many companies on the market that produce numerous follow-up cards, thank-you cards, and contact cards especially designed for networking.

Schedule "reconnection calls" regularly. Such calls enable you to remind the new contacts who you are, where you met them, and what you do, as well as help you stay in touch with your long-term contacts. If you don't follow up with a phone call or letter, you will surely lose many business opportunities.

## Unexpected Referral Sources

S ometimes good referrals come from sources that you least expect. Many business people I meet want to network exclusively with CEOs and corporate presidents. They tell me they don't want to join most business groups, because top executives aren't members. If you're waiting to find a group exclusively for CEOs and top managers, don't hold your breath.

Even when you find such a group, it probably won't help. You see, they don't want you! They're hiding from you. Top business executives insulate themselves from those they think might try to sell them products or services. However, if you develop a word-of-mouth-based business, there's no problem. Through word of mouth you can increase your volume of business because you know a hundred people, who know a hundred people, who in turn know a hundred people, and so on. You are potentially linked to a vast network beyond your own, and you never know who may be in this extended network.

The owner of a drapery business told me about one referral he received. A friend referred an elderly woman to him because the friend thought that he could help her. The woman, who was in her late seventies, had sought the help of many drapery companies to no avail. She wanted to install a pull blind on a small window in the back door of her home; she feared that people going by could look in. The woman explained that normally her son would take care of this but that he was on an extended business trip. No area drapery company would help her because it would be expensive to come out and install a small blind like that. The businessman agreed to help her because she was referred to him by a mutual friend and because she was obviously worried about the situation.

About a month later, the businessman was working in his warehouse/showroom when he noticed an expensive stretch limo pull up in front of his commercial building. Curious, he watched as the chauffeur got out and opened the door for a man dressed in an expensive suit.

The man came into the businessman's showroom and asked for the proprietor. The businessman introduced himself and asked how he could help the gentleman. The man asked whether he remembered the elderly woman for whom he had installed the small blind. The businessman said he remembered her well. The man said that he was impressed that the businessman did this job, because he knew that there was no money in it.

The woman, he said, was his mother, and she had raved about how nice the businessman was and how he had helped her when no one else would. She had instructed her son to use the businessman's service whenever he could. The son told him that he had a new, 6,000-square-foot home by the ocean. He asked the businessman to go out and take measurements, because he wanted to install window coverings throughout the entire house.

The businessman told me that it was the most profitable job he had ever received, and it came from a little old woman who needed a small blind on her back door.

Ironically, the "great referral" you receive is probably not going to come from a CEO, but from someone who *knows* a CEO.

An architect in Las Vegas told me about a window washer he met in one of his networking groups. He said he saw the window washer every week for over nine months before the window washer gave him his first referral. This one referral, however, was worth over $300,000 to the architect!

You never know where a good referral may come from. It may come from a little old lady or a cab driver or a window washer. So don't ignore the possibilities of the contacts that other business people have or can make for you.

> ◆ *The "great referral" you receive is probably not going to come from a CEO, but from someone who* **knows** *a CEO.*

## What If You Get a Bad Referral?

The best way to avoid bad referrals is to tell people when they've given you one. Tell them tactfully, but tell them! If you don't, you'll keep getting bad referrals, and you'll deserve every one of them. I continually run into people who say, "Oh, I can't tell someone that the referral was no good." I say, "You can't afford *not* to tell him." Be direct, and don't apologize. They need to know the referral was bad.

Be positive, and make sure they know it was the referral they gave that was bad, and not their effort. If you expect the best from people, you'll usually get it. If you expect less than the best, you'll usually get that, too. The best way to ensure that you don't get bad referrals is to teach people what you consider

**Worksheet #8**

**THE NOTABLE NETWORKER'S "LEAD TRACKING SYSTEM"**
© Copyright 1987   Ivan R. Misner   Networking For Success, How To Become A Notable Networker

| DATE | LEAD'S NAME | REFERRED BY | CONTACTED LEAD ON (Date) | INTEREST • Hot • Warm • Tepid • Cold | MET LEAD ON (Date) | FOLLOW-UP MEETING(S) ON DATE(S) | STATUS • Closed (sold) • Might Close • No Close | APPROX. VALUE (if closed) | SPINOFFS • Yes (how many) • No |
|------|------------|-------------|-----------|----------|---------|----------|--------|--------|----------|
| | | | | | | | | | |
| | | | | | | | | | |
| | | | | | | | | | |
| | | | | | | | | | |
| | | | | | | | | | |
| | | | | | | | | | |
| | | | | | | | | | |
| | | | | | | | | | |
| | | | | | | | | | |
| | | | | | | | | | |
| | | | | | | | | | |
| | | | | | | | | | |
| | | | | | | | | | |
| | | | | | | | | | |
| | | | | | | | | | |
| | | | | | | | | | |
| | | | | | | | | | |
| | | | | | | | | | |

**Figure 15.1.** Referral Tracking Worksheet

to be a good referral. This differs for each person, and especially for each profession.

For example, some professionals, such as consultants, counselors, and therapists, consider the opportunity to give a speech to a business group a good referral. Others, such as printers, contractors, or florists, normally don't. You cannot assume that everyone knows what kind of referral you're seeking. You need to be very specific about what constitutes a good referral for you.

## TRACKING REFERRALS

**A**n exceptionally effective way of making sure you get good referrals is to monitor the referrals you get. This helps you in many ways. It tells you how often you get referrals, their sources, quality, status, and dollar payoff. Having this information helps you focus on the groups that are giving you the best referrals and reciprocate with the people who are giving you the most referrals.

Figure 15.1 offers an effective referral-tracking system. You use it to record the date you received the referral, who it came from, the date of first contact, how hot it was, the dates you met and followed up, the current status, the approximate value of the referral if it turned into business, and finally, whether it brought any spin-off referrals. All good business executives use raw data such as this to manage their businesses more effectively.

Several parts of the Hand-to-Hand WOMBAT section at the back of this book deal with this chapter. Take the time to review the plan and personalize it to fit your needs. Create your own customer profile questionnaire; consider who you should ask to write testimonial letters for you; evaluate the types of support material you can use for people to remember you; use a structured follow-up program; and begin using a referral tracking system to monitor your word-of-mouth marketing results.

## HOT TIPS AND INSIGHTS

**1** When asking for a referral from an associate or client, use the phrase, "Who do you know who . . . ?" This is an open-ended question that works well. Do not alter the phrase. Other phrases have been tried, but none have produced the desired results.

**2** Have someone else tell a group of people how good your product or service is. This beats anything you can say about yourself. Ask people who have used your products or services to talk about their experience at the next meeting.

**3** Top business executives insulate themselves from those who may try to sell them products or services. Through word of mouth you can still increase your volume of business, because you know a hundred people, who know a hundred people, who in turn know a hundred people, and so on. The great referrals are probably not going to come from a CEO, but from someone who knows a CEO.

**④** If you have an opportunity to distribute your materials, do it. Bring products, samples, brochures, or a presentation book to the business meetings you attend. If people can see, feel, touch, hear, or smell samples of the product or service you provide, they are more likely to use you.

**⑤** Offer a special price or service to the members of your networks. If you can get the members to use you, they are much more likely to refer you.

**⑥** Anyone active in networking groups can benefit by developing a presentation book, taking it to meetings, and making sure it gets circulated.

**⑦** If your product or service is conducive to this approach, tell the members of your network that you accept speaking engagements as bona fide referrals. Ask them to pitch you to the program chair of other organizations they belong to.

**⑧** Meet people outside the meeting context whenever you can. Write cards or letters, send articles that might be of interest, call to check in, and let them know about local business mixers.

**⑨** To get good referrals, tell people when they've given you a bad referral. If you don't, you'll keep getting bad referrals, and you'll deserve every one of them. Teach people what you consider to be a good referral.

**⑩** Monitor the referrals you get. This tells you how often you get referrals, their source, quality, status, and dollar payoff. Having this information helps you focus on individuals and groups that are giving you the best referrals. This allows you to reciprocate with people who are giving you the most referrals.

◆

# Part

# IV

# Relationship
# Building

*A Journey,
Not a Destination*

# Part IV

## Chapter 16
### The Word-of-Mouth Paradigm
*Farming, Not Hunting*

# The Word-of-Mouth Paradigm

## *Farming, Not Hunting*

### WOMBAT REVISITED

**W**ord of mouth is a paradox. Today, everyone recognizes the phrase but few understand how to harness it. I believe, however, that the next generation of business professionals will have a better understanding of this concept. As we move into the 21st century, we are seeing an increasing need for business people to get back to the basics of relationship building. You've discovered in this book that good customer service, while critical to maintaining your existing clients, is not enough to positively impact your word-of-mouth business. As a matter of fact, the W-O-M Factor clearly illustrates that unless you make a concerted effort, word of mouth is likely to have a more negative impact on your business than a positive one.

◆ *There are only four ways to increase your business: advertising, public relations, cold-calling, and word of mouth.*

There are only four ways you can increase your business: advertising, public relations, cold-calling, or the world's best-known marketing secret: word of mouth. If you're going to build your business through word of mouth, then you must break out of that cave-dweller mentality so many business people live by.

Today, more than ever, businesses need an edge over their competition. The answer to this, I believe, is Word-of-Mouth Business Acquisition Tactics, or Hand-to-Hand WOMBAT.

By combining a Powerful, Diverse Network of Contacts and a Positive Message, Delivered Effectively (as shown on page 49 in figure 3.2, the W-O-M Grid) you can realize a very prosperous word-of-mouth-based business. One without the other will not allow you to realize your full potential in word-of-mouth marketing. They are two parts of a whole, combining to make a complete program.

Developing a powerful network involves, among other things, expanding your sphere of influence, utilizing your Contact Spheres, assessing your organizational participation, building connections with multiple networks, and becoming a Hub Firm.

Creating a Positive Message, Delivered Effectively involves, among other things, creating an effective image, learning the skills to deliver your message, developing incentives for people to refer you, using Memory Hooks and LCDs, understanding the Boomerang Effect, and learning the secrets for giving as well as getting referrals.

## FARMING, NOT HUNTING

T he key message of this book is that building your business through word of mouth is more about *farming* than *hunting*. It's about cultivating relationships with other business professionals. As we move toward a new century, we must look back at the enduring values that have served successful businesses well. One of these is trust. We use the services of people and businesses that we trust. Therefore, if we expect others to refer us, we must gain their trust. This is a process — a process of farming, of cultivating relationships that can forge long-lasting referral partnerships.

Unfortunately, in this high-tech society we tend to look for immediate results. Word-of-mouth marketing is not a get-rich-quick scheme or the latest fad. It is a solid foundation for building a successful business. Hence, in order to benefit from this approach, you must understand that building trust takes time. With a bit of persistence, the right effort, and a little time, you can get almost 100 percent of your new business through referrals. Calvin Coolidge once said, "Nothing in the world can take the place of persistence. Talent will not; nothing is more common than unsuccessful men with talent. Genius will not; unrewarded genius is almost a proverb. Education will not; the world is full of educated derelicts."

Persistence and determination are the keys to success in any word-of-mouth effort. Many years ago a man failed in business. The following year he was defeated for a seat in the legislature. The next year he failed in business again. Three years later he suffered a nervous breakdown. Two years after that he was defeated for the speakership of his state's legislature. Two years after that he was defeated for elector. Within three years he was defeated for a seat in the U.S. Congress. Five years later he was defeated for Congress a second time. Seven years later he was defeated for the U.S. Senate. The following year he lost his bid to be vice president. Two years later he was defeated for a seat in the Senate again. Two years after that he was elected president of the United States. The man was Abraham Lincoln.

The message is this: don't give up. Building your referral business takes time, persistence, and a willingness to help others. Many years ago I learned that you can have almost anything you want in business or in life if you're willing to help other people get what they want.

You now have the blueprint for building an incredibly successful referral-based business. If you put these ideas into practice, you will substantially increase your income. The question is, to what extent will you put these ideas into practice? Your word-of-mouth marketing program will be whatever you make of it. But of course, that's the way most things are in business or in life. Take a plain $5 bar of iron and make it into horseshoes and it will be worth around $11. Made into screwdrivers or kitchen knives, the same bar of iron may be worth $250; into needles, around $3,500; into balance springs for watches, almost $250,000! If a simple bar of iron can be worth anywhere from $5 to $250,000, there's no telling what the ideas in this book can be worth to the person who implements them.

Ralph Waldo Emerson once said, "What lies before us and what lies behind us are very little compared to what lies within us." Building a word-of-mouth-based business is all about tapping into the best that lies within us. It requires sharing as well as caring about those with whom we associate. As far as I'm concerned, there is no better way to do business. Word-of-mouth marketing is all about relationship-building in a structured and professional manner. One thing I've learned over the last decade of building my business through word of mouth is this: It's not what you know, or who you know — it's how well you know them that makes the difference.

◆ *It's not what you know, or who you know — it's how well you know them that makes the difference.*

Create a Powerful, Diverse Network of Contacts and provide a Positive Message, Delivered Effectively to people who know and trust you, and success will most certainly be yours.

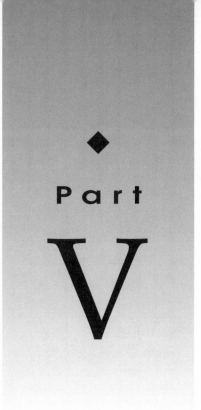

◆

**Part**

# V

# Hand-to-Hand WOMBAT Plan

*A Practical Guide to Word-of-Mouth Marketing*

◆

## Your
# Hand-to-Hand WOMBAT Plan
### and Worksheets

**T**he Hand-to-Hand WOMBAT (Word-of-Mouth Business Acquisition Tactics) Plan focuses on two key concepts that you must incorporate into your business in order to make yourself a master of word-of-mouth marketing. These two components are

1. developing a Powerful, Diverse Network of Contacts, and

2. creating a Positive Message, Delivered Effectively.

The combination of the two results in a prosperous word-of-mouth business:

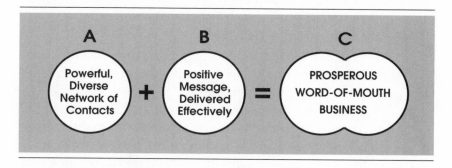

By following the instructions on the left-hand pages that follow and filling in the blanks on the worksheets (the right-hand pages), you will formulate your own WOMBAT Plan. Then you will be ready to strive for the "5/5" (see W-O-M Grid, p. 49, fig. 3.2) and to become a Master at word-of-mouth marketing.

## DEVELOPING A POWERFUL, DIVERSE NETWORK OF CONTACTS

### 1. Compile your contacts.

Assemble all your contacts in one location through whatever medium is easiest for you. It may be a combination of things such as your

| | |
|---|---|
| Computer database | Vendor/client list |
| Mailing lists | Rolodex |
| Business card box | Etc. |

### 2. Categorize your contacts.

Identify each person from the list you've assembled as either a Strong Contact (SC) or a Casual Contact (CC) by marking on the list, card, label, etc.

### 3. Determine your own Contact Sphere.

Contact Spheres are businesses or professions that naturally provide a source of referrals for one another. They have a symbiotic, compatible, noncompetitive relationship with one another, such as a lawyer, CPA, financial planner, and banker.

Begin to make contact with the professions you've listed. Agree to have a reciprocal referral relationship with the ones you feel you can work with best.

### 4. Plan to become a Hub Firm.

A Hub Firm is the key business in a constellation of businesses tethered to one another to make the most of each firm's products, services, or expertise.

List the types of firms that you should build partnerships or alliances with to better enable you to serve your market. These include businesses that fall within your Contact Sphere; however, they may include other businesses, such as competitors with different specialties.

Once you've listed these companies, set appointments with each to begin the relationship-building process. See if there are any joint-venture projects that you can conduct with them on a trial basis.

## WORKSHEETS

1. **Compile your contacts.**
   List resources from which you compiled your contact list:

   1.                      4.

   2.                      5.

   3.                      6.

2. **Categorize your contacts.**

   Number of Strong Contacts:

   Number of Casual Contacts:

3. **Determine your own Contact Sphere.**
   Your profession:

   List related professions (Contact Spheres):

   1.                      5.

   2.                      6.

   3.                      7.

   4.                      8.

4. **Plan to become a Hub Firm.**
   List types of firms that should be your allies:

   1.                      5.

   2.                      6.

   3.                      7.

   4.                      8.

### 5a. Establish contact.

Don't become a cave dweller. Set goals for the number of appointments you will establish with the people you want to have in your Contact Sphere or will build an alliance with as a Hub Firm.

### 5b. Set attendance goals.

Establish goals for the number of business groups you will attend each month for the next three months.

### 6. Diversify your networks.

The selection process is very important. Don't let chance decide where you're going to spend your time and efforts. Remember, the key is to diversify your activities. One type of business organization will not serve all your needs. Therefore, you should consciously select a well-rounded mix of groups. Try to avoid being in more than one group per category. If you have associates, partners, or employees, take their participation into account when deciding what groups you need to become active in.

    a.   Based on the types of groups shown opposite, list the names of the ones that you now belong to.

    b.   List the groups that you are not a member of but would like to consider.

    c.   Find out when each group meets, write down its location, and visit its next meeting.

    d.   With each group, find out the following information:

        1.   How long has this group been in existence?

        2.   How many members does it have?

        3.   What is the quality of the membership?

        4.   Is it affiliated with a national or international group?

        5.   How focused is the group on its objectives?

        6.   How structured are the meetings?

        7.   How much does it cost?

        8.   How often are the meetings?

        9.   What do other members say about the group?

        10.  What is your overall impression of the group?

**5a. Establish contact.**

Number of appointments:

Next 30 days:          60 days:          90 days:

**5b. Set attendance goals.**

Number of business groups you will attend:

Next 30 days:          60 days:          90 days:

**6.  Plan group membership.**

List (a) the names of the following types of groups that you now belong to and (b) those you would like to consider:

1. Casual-Contact          a.
   Networks:               b.
2. Strong-Contact          a.
   Networks:               b.
3. Community-service       a.
   groups:                 b.
4. Professional            a.
   associations:           b.
5. Social/business         a.
   groups:                 b.
6. Women's business        a.
   organizations:          b.

c. Record date and location of next meeting:
   (Use extra sheets of paper as necessary.)

d. Answer 10 questions about each group:
   (Use extra sheets of paper as necessary.)

   1.                        6.
   2.                        7.
   3.                        8.
   4.                        9.
   5.                       10.

## CREATING A POSITIVE MESSAGE, DELIVERED EFFECTIVELY

1. Describe the identity you wish to create.

2. List the key topics for your next four press releases.

3. What news article reprints do you have?

4. Collateral materials.
   Check off the collateral materials you now have or want. Begin compiling the ones you want but have not created yet.

1. **Identity you wish to create for your business:**

2. **Key topics for your next four press releases:**

   1.                    3.

   2.                    4.

3. **News article reprints:**

4. **Collateral materials:**

   Have Want
   ☐ ☐    Testimonial letters from satisfied customers
   ☐ ☐    Articles in which you're mentioned
   ☐ ☐    Published articles by you
   ☐ ☐    Unpublished articles by you
   ☐ ☐    A one- or two-page faxable flyer
   ☐ ☐    Audio or video cassettes you've produced
   ☐ ☐    Published new-product announcements/press releases
   ☐ ☐    Copies of display advertisements that you've used
   ☐ ☐    Text from radio or TV advertisements that you've run
   ☐ ☐    A list of your memberships and affiliations
   ☐ ☐    Product catalogs
   ☐ ☐    Brochures, circulars, or data sheets
   ☐ ☐    Question-and-answer sheets
   ☐ ☐    Annual report, capability statement, or prospectus
   ☐ ☐    Newsletters or news-type letters you use
   ☐ ☐    Your motto, mission statement, or service pledge
   ☐ ☐    Sample client or customer proposals and bid sheets
   ☐ ☐    Survey results by you or others
   ☐ ☐    Presentation notes, slides, or overheads
   ☐ ☐    Marketing letters you wrote to clients
   ☐ ☐    Generic materials developed by your association
   ☐ ☐    Articles on trends affecting your target niche
   ☐ ☐    Posters, banners, display materials used at trade shows
   ☐ ☐    Photos of your office facilities, equipment, products (with staff, clients, etc.)
   ☐ ☐    Photos of your key customer's office facilities, equipment, products
   ☐ ☐    Photos of you and your staff
   ☐ ☐    Other:

### 5. Networking tools.

Assemble the networking tools listed opposite.

### 6. Incentive program.

Assemble a focus group expressly to develop an incentive plan for your business. Make sure to include incentives for all the people relevant to your business.

### 7. Incentives.

a. List the ideas that the group (and/or you) liked the most. Give a brief description of each kind of incentive — who qualifies, what is the incentive, etc.

b. List the things that you need to do to begin incorporating these incentives into your business.

### 8. Memberships.

List (a) the organizations that you belong to and (b) a position corresponding with each (i.e., Ambassador, Visitor Host, etc.) that will give you more exposure or an opportunity to meet others.

### 9. Memory Hooks.

Create at least one or two Memory Hooks for your business. A Memory Hook is a brief, ear-catching phrase in your presentation that so vividly describes what you do that people will be able to visualize it in their mind's eye; in other words, you hook your audience with your presentation.

5. **Networking tools.**

   Assemble the following networking tools:
   - [ ] A professionally made name badge
   - [ ] Card holders for each suit, briefcase, purse, etc., to carry your business cards
   - [ ] A card file to carry other people's business cards
   - [ ] A contact management system or computer program
   - [ ] A collateral material package

6. **Incentive program.**

   Members of your focus group:

   Clients/customers/patients:

   Employees:

   Associates:

   Others:

7. **Incentives.**

   a. Best incentives:     b. Incorporating:

   1.

   2.

   3.

8. **Memberships.**

   a. Organization:     b. Position:

   1.

   2.

   3.

   4.

   5.

9. **Memory Hooks.**

   1.

   2.

### 10. List lowest common denominators (LCDs).

List some LCDs that your business shares with any relevant areas listed opposite.

### 11. Prepare a brief introduction.

List the information indicated opposite for use when you introduce yourself to a networking group.

### 12. Work your networks.

List some people or businesses that you do business with or refer others to, who are not reciprocating, then invite someone from that company out to lunch or to one of your business groups.

### 10. Lowest common denominators (LCDs).

Specific products/services:

Target markets:

Benefits of your products/services:

Your and/or your company's qualifications:

Specific case studies:

### 11. Prepare a brief introduction.

Your name:

A brief description of your business or profession:

A Memory Hook:

A benefit statement or LCD using one particular product or service you offer (what you do that helps others):

### 12. Work your networks.

1.

2.

3.

4.

5.

6.

### 13. Expand your networks.

List people representing professions that you would like to do business with or refer others to. Call them and set appointments to get together for lunch.

### 14. Look ahead.

Most important, take another look at the W-O-M Grid (p. 49, fig. 3.2) and think about where you are today on the grid. After reading this book and working with your Hand-to-Hand WOMBAT Plan for three months, check the grid once more and see how far you've progressed.

Remember: building your business through word of mouth is a journey, not a destination. It is something you must continually work on over the years.

## 13. Expand your networks.

People representing professions you would like to do business with or refer others to:

Name:                    Phone number:

1.

2.

3.

4.

5.

6.

7.

8.

## 14. Look ahead.

# BIBLIOGRAPHY

## Books

Baber, Anne, and Lynn Waymon. *Great Connections.* Manassas Park, Virginia: Impact Publications, 1992.

Bjorseth, Lillian. *Breakthrough Networking.* Lisle, Illinois: Duoforce, 1996.

Blanchard, Ken, and Robert Lorber. *Putting the One-Minute Manager to Work.* New York: William Morrow and Co., 1984.

Bly, Bob. *The Copywriter's Handbook.* New York: Owl, 1992.

Boe, Anne. *Networking Success.* Encinitas, California: Seaside Press, 1994.

Boe, Anne, and Bettie B. Youngs. *Is Your "Net" Working?* New York: Wiley & Sons, 1989.

Burg, Bob. *Endless Referrals: Network Your Everyday Contacts into Sales.* New York: McGraw-Hill, 1994.

Byrum-Robinson, B., and D. Womeldroff. "Networking Skills Inventory." In *The 1990 Annual: Developing Human Resources,* edited by J. William Pfeiffer, San Diego: University Associates, 1990.

Cashman, Kevin J. Networking: *Building Relationships, Building Success.* St. Paul, Minnesota: Devine Multi-Media Publishing, 1994.

Cates, Bill. *Unlimited Referrals.* Wheaton, Maryland: Thunder Hill Press, 1996.

Craig, Robert L., ed. *Training and Development Handbook.* New York: McGraw-Hill, 1987.

Daniels, Aubrey. *How to Bring Out the Best in People.* New York: McGraw-Hill, 1993.

Davidson, Jeff. *Marketing on a Shoestring.* New York: Wiley & Sons, 1988.

Davis, Robert, and Laura Miller. *Total Quality Introductions* (audio-cassette). Upland, California: Robert Davis Associates, 1991.

Edwards, Paul, Sarah Edwards, and Laura Douglas. *Getting Business to Come to You.* Los Angeles: Jeremy P. Tarcher, 1991.

Edwards, Paul, and Sarah Edwards. *Best Home Businesses for the '90s.* Los Angeles: Jeremy P. Tarcher, 1991.

Fisher, Donna. *People Power: 12 Power Principles to Enrich Your Business, Career & Personal Networks.* Austin: Bard Press, 1995.

Fisher, Donna, and Sandy Vilas. *Power Networking: 55 Secrets for Personal & Professional Success.* Austin, Texas: MountainHarbour Publications, 1992.

Fraser, George. *Success Runs in Our Race.* New York: Avon Books, 1994.

Holtz, Herman. *Great Promo Pieces.* New York: Wiley & Sons, 1991.

Henderson, Robyn. *Networking for Success.* Collaroy Plateau, Australia: Murray Child & Company, 1992, 1998.

Jolley, Willie. *It Only Takes a Minute to Change Your Life.* New York: St. Martin's Press, 1997.

Krannich, Robert L., and Caryl Rae Krannich. *Network Your Way to Job and Career Success.* Alexandria, Virginia: Impact Publications, 1989.

Linn, Susann. *Directory of Orange County Networking Organizations, 1999 edition.* Corona Del Mar, California: Susann Linn, 1998.

Mackay, Harvey. *Dig Your Well Before You're Thirsty.* New York: Doubleday, 1997.

Misner, Ivan R. *Networking for Success.* Claremont, California: Business Paradigm Productions, 1987.

Misner, Ivan R. *Seven Second Marketing: How to Use Memory Hooks to Make You Instantly Stand Out in a Crowd.* Austin: Bard Press, 1996.

Misner, Ivan R., and Robert Davis. *Business by Referral: A Sure-Fire Way to Generate New Business.* Austin: Bard Press, 1998.

Naisbitt, John. *Megatrends: Ten New Directions Transforming Our Lives.* New York: Warner Books, 1982.

Naisbitt, John, and Patricia Aburdenem. *Re-Inventing the Corporation.* New York: Warner Books, 1985.

Office of the President. *The State of Small Business: A Report of the President.* Washington, D.C.: U.S. Government Printing Office, 1987.

Osborn, Alex. *Applied Imagination.* New York: Charles Scribner, 1953.

Peters, Tom, *Thriving on Chaos.* New York: Alfred A. Knopf, 1987.

Ries, Al, and Jack Trout. *Positioning: The Battle for Your Mind.* New York: McGraw-Hill, 1981.

RoAne, Susan. *How to Work a Room.* New York: Warner Books, 1991.

RoAne, Susan. *The Secrets of Savvy Networking.* New York: Warner Books, 1993.

Rogers, Everett M., and D. Lawrence Kincaid. *Communication Networks: Toward a New Paradigm for Research.* New York: Free Press, 1981.

Scheele, Adele. *Skills for Success.* New York: William Morrow and Co., 1979.

Sheer, Mark. *Referrals.* Mission Viejo, California: Sheer Seminars, 1993.

Small Business Administration. *1988 Annual Report.* Washington, D.C.: U.S. Government Printing Office, 1988.

Stanley, Thomas. *Marketing to the Affluent.* Homewood, Illinois: BusinessOne-Irwin, 1988.

Sukenick, Ron. *Networking Your Way to Success.* Dubuque, Iowa: Kendall/Hunt Publishing Co., 1995.

Toffler, Alvin. *Power Shift: Knowledge, Wealth, and Violence at the Edge of the 21st Century.* New York: Bantam Books, 1990.

Toffler, Alvin. *The Third Wave.* New York: William Morrow and Co., 1980.

U.S. Chamber of Commerce. *1992 Survey of Local Chambers of Commerce.* Washington, D.C.: Office of Chamber of Commerce Relations, 1992.

U.S. Department of Commerce. *Enterprise Statistics.* Washington, D.C.: U.S. Government Printing Office, 1977.

Wilson, Jerry R. *Word-of-Mouth Marketing.* New York: John Wiley & Sons, 1991.

Woods, Donald R., and Shirley D. Ormerod. *Networking: How to Enrich Your Life and Get Things Done.* San Diego, California: Pfeiffer & Company, 1993.

## Periodicals

Applegate, Jane. "Networking Clubs: Business Over the Eggs Benedict." *Los Angeles Times,* 29 May 1989, Business section.

Baber, Anne, and Lynn Waymon. "No-Nonsense Networking." *Your Company* (Summer 1993): 34–37.

Babi, R. "Network Your Way to Net Profits." *Business News* (Spring 1993): 31.

Bell, S. "Power Networking." *Black Enterprise 16* (February 1986): 111–14, 132.

Bonacich, P. "Communication Dilemmas in Social Networks: An Experimental Study." *American Sociological Review* 55, no. 3 (June 1990): 448–60.

Boudette, Neal E. "Networks to Dismantle Old Structures." *Industry Week* 238, no. 2 (16 January 1989): 27–31.

Burg, Bob. "Join the (Networking) Club." *Real Estate Today* 25, no. 9 (October 1992): 48–49.

Byrd, Richard E. "Corporate Leadership Skills: A New Synthesis." *Organizational Dynamics* 16 (Summer 1987): 34–43.

Carlson, Jayne. "Building Trust and a Client Base Through Networking." *Home-Office Computing* 9, no. 9 (September 1991): 41–42.

Chazin, Christopher. "Valley-Based Network Blossoms." (Ontario, Calif.) *Daily Bulletin,* 26 January 1992, sec. B.

Corbett, Katie. "Networking Called 'Serious Business.'" *Antelope Valley Press,* 18 April 1989, C-5.

Davis, Robert. "A Study of the Relationship Between Networking Skills Inventory Scores and the Quantity and Quality of Leads Exchanged Between Members of 'The Network.'" Master's thesis, University of San Francisco, 1991.

Emshwiller, John R. "Networking Firms Offer Contacts for Sale." *The Wall Street Journal,* 8 February 1991, sec. B.

Erdman, Ken. "Does Your Business Card Really Mean Business?" *The Rotarian* (August 1989): 12–17.

Farris, Chris. "This Network Means Business." *Carlsbad Magazine* (February 1990): 21.

Fombrun, Charles J. "Attributions of Power Across a Social Network." *Human Relations* 36 (1983): 493–508.

Good, Bill. "Networking: The Old Way Becomes the New Way." *Research* (September 1991): 24–26.

Grayson, Jackson. "Networking by Computer." *The Futurist* 18 (June 1984): 15.

Grieco, Margaret S., and D. M. Hosking. "Networking, Exchange, and Skill." *International Studies of Management and Organization* 17 (1987): 75–88.

Haddon, Margie. "Build Your Business through a Networking Club." *Home-Office Computing* 9, no. 12 (December 1991): 24, 26.

Helgensen, S. "The Truth about Networking." *Glamour* 83, no. 9 (September 1985): 236.

Hellgren, B., and J. Stjernberg. "Networks: An Analytical Tool for Understanding Complex Decision Processes." *International Studies of Management and Organization* 17 (1987): 88–103.

Hill, Don. "A Hot New Trend That Builds Business the Old Fashioned Way: Networking." *Independent Business* (September–October 1990): 30–32.

Hine, Virginia. "Networks in a Global Society." *The Futurist* 18 (June 1984): 11–13.

Hosking, D. M. "Organizing, Leadership, and Skillful Process." *Journal of Management Studies* 25, no. 2 (March 1988): 147–66.

James, Eric. "How to Build and Improve Business Networking Skills." *California Real Estate* (July–August 1987): 28–31.

Jarillo, Carlos. "On Strategic Networks." *Strategic Management Journal* 9, no. 1 (January–February 1988): 31.

Kanter, Rosabeth Moss. "The Middle Manager as Innovator." *Harvard Business Review* 60, no. 4 (1982): 95–105.

Keil, Jeffrey. "Professionals Network Their Way to Success." (Tulare, Calif.) *Advance-Register*, 20 March 1990, 12.

Kiechell, Walter. "The Care and Feeding of Contacts." *Fortune* (8 February 1982): 119.

Kotter, John P. "What Effective Managers Do." *Harvard Business Review* 60, no. 6 (November–December 1982): 156–67.

Leigh, Bruce. "Winning Webs." *International Management* 43, nos. 7, 8 (July–August 1988): 26–28.

Lipnack, Jessica, and Jeffery Stamps. "A Network Model." *The Futurist* 21 (1987): 23–26.

McGuire, Jean. "A Dialectical Analysis of Interorganizational Networks." *Journal of Management* 14, no. 1 (March 1988): 109.

McInnis, Noel. "Networking: A Way to Manage Our Changing World?" *The Futurist* 18 (June 1984): 9–10.

Melia, Marilyn K. "Power Source: Networking Groups Let Home-Based Entrepreneurs Stay Well Connected." *Chicago Tribune*, 14 April 1994.

Misner, Ivan R. "Business Development Networks: An Exploratory Study." Ph.D. diss., University of Southern California, 1993.

Misner, Ivan. "Surviving the Squeeze of a Tight Economy." *Indianapolis C.E.O.* (November–December 1990): 10.

Nelson, Reed E. "The Strength of Strong Ties: Social Networks and Intergroup Conflict in Organizations." *Academy of Management Journal* 32, no. 2 (1989): 377–402.

Owchar, Nick. "Network Chapters Help Create Area Business Contacts," *San Gabriel Valley Tribune*, 25 June 1988, Business section.

Singer, Penny. "Small Businesses Find Networking Pays." *The New York Times*, 26 July 1992.

Smith, P. J. "Networking: What It Is, What It Can Do for You, How to Do It." *Vital Speeches of the Day* 49 (September 1983): 712–3.

Sonnenberg, Frank K. "How to Reap the Benefits of Networking." *Journal of Business Strategy* 11, no. 1 (January–February 1990): 59–63.

Tichy, Noel M., and Charles J. Fombrun. "Network Analysis in Organizational Settings." *Human Relations* 32, no. 11 (November 1979): 923–65.

Tichy, Noel M., M. L. Tushman, and C. J. Fombrun. "Social Network Analysis for Organizations." *Academy of Management Review* 4, no. 4 (October 1979): 507–19.

Waymon, Lynn. "Business Networking Puts Money in the Bank." *Washington Business Journal* (28 May–3 June 1993).

Yanagida, Ichikazu. "The Business Network: A Powerful and Challenging Business Tool." *Journal of Business Venturing* 7, no. 5 (September 1992): 341–6.

Zack, Ian. "'The Network' Opens New Doors." *Springfield* (Connecticut) *Connection*, 13 March 1991, 13.

# INDEX

# About **BNI**

**B** usiness Network Int'l., or BNI, was founded by Dr. Ivan Misner in 1985 as a way for business people to generate referrals in a structured, professional environment. The organization now has tens of thousands of members on almost every continent of the world. Since its inception, members of BNI have passed millions of referrals, generating billions of dollars for the participants.

The primary purpose of the organization is to pass qualified business referrals to the members. The philosophy of BNI may be summed up in two simple words: Givers Gain. If you give business to people, you will get business from them. BNI allows only one person per profession to join a chapter. The program is designed for business people to develop long-term relationships, thereby creating a basis for trust and, inevitably, referrals. The mission of the organization is to teach business professionals that the word-of-mouth process is more about farming than it is hunting: it's about the cultivation of professional relationships in a structured business environment for the mutual benefit of all.

You can contact BNI on the Internet at bni@bni.com or visit our Web site at www.bni.com.

# Information Order Form

*Please send me information on*

- ☐ A BNI chapter near me
- ☐ Having Dr. Misner as a speaker
- ☐ Audiotapes on networking
- ☐ How to obtain additional copies of this book or other works by Dr. Misner

Name _____

Company _____ Phone (___)_____

Address _____

City _____ State ____ Zip_____

*To receive the information listed above, please send this form to*

BNI — Business Network Int'l.
545 College Commerce Way
Upland, CA 91786-4377
909-608-7575 (inside So. Cal.), 800-825-8286 (outside So. Cal.)
Fax: 909-608-7676, e-mail: bni@bni.com

*Please feel free to send your comments on this book to Dr. Misner at the address listed above.*